VERHANDELINGEN

VAN HET KONINKLIJK INSTITUUT
VOOR TAAL-, LAND- EN VOLKENKUNDE

76

C. CH. GOSLINGA

CURAÇAO AND GUZMÁN BLANCO

A CASE STUDY OF SMALL POWER POLITICS
IN THE CARIBBEAN

'S-GRAVENHAGE - MARTINUS NIJHOFF 1975

CURAÇAO AND GUZMÁN BLANCO

To Marian

VERHANDELINGEN

VAN HET KONINKLIJK INSTITUUT
VOOR TAAL-, LAND- EN VOLKENKUNDE

76

C. CH. GOSLINGA

CURAÇAO AND GUZMÁN BLANCO

A CASE STUDY OF SMALL POWER POLITICS IN THE CARIBBEAN

'S-GRAVENHAGE - MARTINUS NIJHOFF 1975

The publication of this study was made possible by a grant from STICUSA, the Netherlands Foundation for Cultural Cooperation with Surinam and the Netherlands Antilles.

I.S.B.N. 90 247 1836 8

PREFACE

This monograph explores a critical phase in the history of the Dutch colony of Curaçao and its development of political relations with Venezuela. Tensions and conflicts growing out of these relations acquired an extra Caribbean dimension with the involvement of the Netherlands in a region she had previously neglected. In concentrating on the political aspects of Curaçao's role in this complex entanglement of interests and influences, the author is only too aware that he has excluded other relevant matters in favor of a more single-minded, monographic approach. These include the relationship between legal and illegal trade and its influence upon the economy of both the island and the Venezuelan republic; the existence of a powerful merchant-class in the colony; and the rise of what might be termed a national consciousness in Venezuela at the same time the Dutch island was becoming aware of its almost complete dependence on a distant metropolis unfamiliar with Curaçao's problems and needs.

On the other hand, the essence of any monograph, its strength and perhaps its weakness, is to be found in just such a narrow focus. And while political problems may not be the most pressing ones in an international competition of interests, they are more often than not the decisive ones. Hence, the author's case study approach.

Primary source materials are to be found in The Hague, where the *Algemeen Rijks Archief* (ARA, Government Archives), possesses an extensive collection of documents related to Venezuelan affairs, catalogued as A-128, *Venezolaanse Zaken*. Documents are organized in chronological sub-collections, running from about 1870 to 1908. Additional information was obtained from the extensive *Holanda Dossier* of the *Ministerio de Relaciones Exteriores* (MRE, Ministry of Foreign Affairs, Caracas), which is divided into topical sub-collections. Whenever identical data are to be found in both archives, citation is made only to ARA.

Other important research sources were for Venezuela the *Libro Amarillo* and the *Gaceta Oficial*; and for the Netherlands the *Nederlandsche Staatscourant* (Official Dutch Gazette), the *Handelingen van de Tweede*

Kamer der Staten Generaal (Activities of the Second Chamber of the States General), and the *Koloniale Verslagen* (Colonial Reports). Extensive use was also made of the contemporary press: *La Opinión Nacional,* mouthpiece of the Guzmán Blanco regime; a Dutch paper, *Dagblad van Zuid-Holland en 's-Gravenhage,* which featured overseas affairs; and Curaçao's own *De Curaçaosche Courant, El Imparcial,* and *Civilisadó.* Important pamphlets relating to the topic include *El Evangelio Liberal, Holanda y Venezuela,* and *Is Curaçao te koop?* (Is Curaçao for sale?).

My thanks to Mrs. Sandra F. McGee and Ms. B. A. Cohen Stuart for editing the text.

Cornelis Ch. Goslinga

CONTENTS

1. PROLOGUE

It was a Saturday morning at the end of January, 1870. The Hendrikplein in Willemstad lay under a burning tropical glare. A strong breeze and scattered shade under the few languishing trees gave only partial relief from the sun. Most of the buildings surrounding the *plein* lacked the dignity of those on its southern side, where the newly constructed Temple Emanu-El represented faith and the courthouse with its neo-classical tympanon and broad entrance reflected cool, austere justice.

Heat waves gave a shimmering look to the houses around the *plein* and along the Breedestraat. To one side stood venerable Fort Amsterdam, which had defended St. Ann Bay, the main port entrance of Curaçao, for almost two centuries. From the center of the fort rose the governor's palace, its rooftop flag signalling that the governor was in residence. Far off, one could see the heat-distorted outline of Fort Nassau on Sablica hill at the other end of St. Ann Bay, the island's current defense.

Four dark-haired men in white shirtsleeves and black trousers appeared in front of the courthouse. Three were middle-aged, one of them quite tall. The fourth was much older. Their gaze shifted from where the yellow walls of Fort Amsterdam shut out the sea to the gray menacing strength of Fort Nassau and its advertisement of the Dutch presence in the Caribbean: a red, white, and blue banner flapping in the wind.

The four men walked slowly up the courthouse steps and disappeared. Inside, a dark usher brought them to a door bearing the sign *Procureur Generaal* (Attorney General) and bade them enter.

Salomon Senior, acting Attorney General of the Colony *Curaçao en Onderhoorigheden* (Curaçao and Dependencies), was a descendant of Jewish exiles who had long ago found refuge at Curaçao under the Dutch flag. They and many other Jewish families had prospered there in commercial activities, at times licit and at other times including smuggling.

Senior was uneasy over the message he had to give to Antonio

Guzmán Blanco, his father Antonio Leocadio Guzmán, and the other two Venezuelans. He rose immediately from behind his enormous mahogany desk to greet them.

"Por favor, siéntense Ustedes, señores."

The governor of the colony, Abraham Mathieu de Rouville, had personally shown Senior the orders from The Hague for the expulsion of the Venezuelans. De Rouville had protested, strongly for a subordinate, but the Minister for the Colonies had insisted that "the residence of the Guzmans in Curaçao was contrary to neutrality." [1] Thus, against his better judgment, the governor was carrying out instructions.[2]

The Attorney General referred the Guzmans to another meeting the previous November, when they had been warned, under penalty of expulsion under an island regulation of 1866, not to engage in political or military plotting against the government in Caracas. They listened silently.

"What is the proof for the present accusation?" asked the older man.

Senior shook his head. "I showed you those damaging letters in November, remember?"

"It must be that impossible Rolandus," said Guzmán Blanco, the tall one.

Senior read the order of expulsion, effective February 15. When he had finished, the father spoke again.

"Do you believe, señor, that we have violated any law?"

"Perhaps not Venezuelan law. But you have violated our laws."

"In 1848, when I enjoyed your hospitality," the older man persisted, "nothing was done against me."

"We have a new regulation," the Attorney General answered quietly. "If it had been in force in 1848, we would have had to do the same."

"You said that the deadline was February 15?" Guzmán Blanco asked.

The Attorney General nodded.

"Would you permit me to leave secretly, before that date?"

"Your reason, please, señor Guzmán Blanco."

"Then my enemies won't know when or where to expect me."

The Attorney General thought for a moment. "Each ship leaving port is required to register its passengers, but this can be arranged as long as you keep me informed."

Guzmán Blanco looked relieved. The brief ceremony was over. Once again the four men stood on the hot cobbles of the Hendrikplein. They walked leisurely to St. Ann Bay, crossed it in a small ferry, and then walked up Otrabanda's main street toward the huge mansion still known today as the Casa Guzmán Blanco.

The order of expulsion was directed against Antonio Leocadio Guzmán, his son Antonio Guzmán Blanco, and their supporters, Martín J. Sanabria and Hilario Parra. The accusation: conspiracy against the Venezuelan government.

The Guzmans were prominent liberals from Venezuela in exile. When they had been deported, on August 20, 1869, the Venezuelan commercial house of Boulton had put a ship in La Guaira at their disposal, but instead they had chosen to use the Dutch schooner *Midas,* owned by the Jewish house of J. A. Jesurun & Son of Curaçao.[3] Other Venezuelan refugees had followed them to Curaçao in the course of the year.[4]

By the time the February 15 deadline had passed, three of the four men were gone from the island — the elder Guzmán was excused because of sickness and did not leave until May 1. The *Curaçaosche Courant* had a premonition: "We will trust that our fear ... that Venezuela will avenge the expulsion of Venezuelans from this colony, does not materialize."[5]

But the *Curaçaosche Courant* soon found that it was all too good a prophet.[6]

2. THE SITUATION

Political and economic relations between Venezuela and the non-Hispanic Caribbean, in particular the island of Curaçao, have been delicate since the war for independence. In colonial times, when Venezuela was a captaincy-general, the strategically-located island served as a slave market and warehouse, providing the Spanish colony with a much-needed black labor force and many commodities which Spain was unable to provide. These trade relations, although largely illicit, had a great impact on Curaçao and were the source of its prosperity in the seventeenth and eighteenth centuries.

This idyllic situation ended when the Spanish-American continent began to revolt. After the English occupation of the Curaçao islands (1807-1816), the Dutch discovered to their dismay that trade had moved away from Willemstad to St. Thomas in the Virgin group.[1] Contacts on the mainland had been reduced to Coro and Maracaibo; return cargoes contained only a few goatskins or other hides and some species of wood.[2]

A revival of the former trade was difficult to accomplish for several reasons. First, the Netherlands was unresigned to the loss of the Guiana colony to Great Britain. Amsterdam merchants had invested huge sums in the former Dutch possession, and their commercial interests in the West were suffering. Second, long after all the other Caribbean powers had opened their ports to free trade, the Dutch government still failed to recognize the changed circumstances and maintained until 1827 a six percent duty on commodities not originating in the mother country. For more than a decade this tariff policy was the main obstacle to restoring commercial relations between Willemstad and the new republic of Venezuela. A third reason for bad feeling was the unfortunate Dutch decision to side with the peninsula in Spain's conflict with her American colonies.[3]

Thus Curaçao's role as a commercial intermediary between Venezuela and the outside world was almost completely eliminated. It took The Hague some time to discover what was amiss, as political developments in the years 1816 to 1822 only increased the problems caused by the

Dutch attitude. Until 1822, while siding with Spain, the Dutch not only closed Curaçao's ports to ships of Venezuelan patriots, but even stretched their sympathies so far as to convoy Spanish merchant ships threatened by Venezuelan or Gran Colombian privateers. Spanish troops fighting in Venezuela and Colombia depended mainly on provisions coming from the Dutch island.[4]

The Battle of Carabobo in 1822 produced a vital change: the Dutch Foreign Office finally realized that the Spanish cause in America was lost. Following the example set by the United States and Great Britain, the Dutch government adopted a policy of strict neutrality, conferring on patriots the so-called rights of belligerents. Even Spain had recognized those rights as early as 1820 in the Treaty of Trujillo.

This neutrality policy clearly revealed the change in The Hague's analysis of the situation. It was strictly followed until 1827, when a new effort was launched to break the impasse in Curaçao's trade. The island was now declared a free port and consuls were appointed in the ports of Gran Colombia (whose government considered this action *de facto* recognition of her independence). A treaty of commerce and friendship followed in 1829, but shortly afterwards Gran Colombia collapsed and the recently-concluded treaty became a dead letter.[5]

A new period began with fresh negotiations in 1830. The independent Venezuelan republic accepted the Gran Colombian treaty with minor revisions. Finally, relations between Venezuela and the Netherlands and her colonial dependencies were normalized.[6]

This normalization of relations did not eliminate the complex set of problems which played such an important role in the existing situation. Curaçao's geographical location assumed a vital importance because of the instability of successive governments in the Land of Bolívar. From the outset, opponents of any Caracas regime found an excellent refuge close at hand in Willemstad, where they could frame conspiracies, buy military supplies, and launch attacks against almost any point of Venezuela's poorly-defended coast. In other words, Curaçao soon became the headquarters of Venezuelan rebels, sharing this unenviable role with Trinidad. If the rebels achieved their goals, the in-party of Caracas would be ousted, exiled, and the same game would continue, roles reversed.

As a result of this development, the history of the relations between Venezuela and Curaçao was largely dominated by a litany of complaints originating in Caracas and noticeably effective in pressuring the Dutch colonial government's policy of granting refuge to political exiles.

Of course, Caracas always conveniently forgot that this very policy had enabled its own party to rise to power.[7] Continuous, irritating agitation dramatized this unhappy relationship: seizure of Dutch ships, confiscation of Dutch property, and demonstrations against Dutch subjects living in Venezuela became common occurrences. The Dutch colonial government reacted with remarkable restraint in issuing regulations to control the export of war materiel which failed to satisfy contending Venezuelan power elites.[8] Thus a vicious circle of strain and tension between the island and the continental republic began. Negotiations, promises, treaties, ruptures of diplomatic and commercial relations, privateering, naval demonstrations, and reconciliations succeeded one another. These and other manifestations of enmity and amity reached an emotional peak during the years when Antonio Guzmán Blanco controlled the fate of Venezuela and gave his country a new sense of direction.

3. EXPULSION

In 1863 a devastating civil war which brought Venezuela to the verge of economic collapse ended with the victory of the Liberal or Federalist Party, also called the Yellows, under General Juan C. Falcón. The profitable trade in the smuggling of arms and ammunition, in which the commercial house of J. A. Jesurun & Son had figured significantly, appeared to have ended. That Dutch subjects were deeply involved in this trade caused The Hague and its agent, the Governor of Curaçao, some discomfiture. With the rise of Falcón to the presidency of Venezuela, however, the Dutch Second Chamber was informed that good relations between the Republic and Curaçao had been restored.[1]

Unfortunately, this assurance was too optimistic. Falcón, proving himself incompetent, fell from power. Rioting and rebellion erupted again and the conservative faction, the Blues, gained control. Almost from its beginning, the new government issued a long list of complaints: Venezuelan (Yellow) exiles were conspiring in Willemstad; the governor of the island was permitting the sale of arms and ammunition to its enemies. These complaints found their way to The Hague where a change of Cabinet had brought a new man, E. de Waal, to the Ministry for the Colonies. Unfamiliar with the situation, he doubtlessly over-relied on the suggestions of the Dutch chargé d'affaires in Caracas, F. D. G. Rolandus.[2] The result of his lack of experience soon became tragically apparent.

The Governor of Curaçao, De Rouville, was a man whose integrity and ability were beyond doubt. He had served the colony for more than ten years as chief of police and Attorney General, and in 1866 King William III had appointed him governor. He was perhaps more familiar with the colony's problems than anyone else. It was during his term as governor that relations with Venezuela took a fatal turn.

The Governor of Curaçao and Dependencies had modest executive power and controlled the Colonial *Raad* (Council) to a certain extent by appointing five of its thirteen members. In reality, however, he was nothing more than an agent of the Minister for the Colonies in The Hague,[3] a not exceptional position in those days. Thus when De Waal ordered De Rouville to expel the most prominent Venezuelan exiles, all leading liberals, the governor was forced to obey.

Yet De Rouville hesitated. The removal, perhaps forcible, of political exiles from Curaçao was totally contrary to island tradition. The principles of broad tolerance, religious as well as political, culminating in a laissez-faire economic policy, were deeply embedded in the Dutch national character and had taken firm root in the colony. Fleeing from intolerance, refugees had flocked to Curaçao from Cuba, Haiti, Santo Domingo, and Venezuela. The precedent of an expulsion was a frightening prospect for colonial authorities. Expulsion had been anticipated, however, in an as-yet untested insular regulation of 1866.

When Antonio Guzmán Blanco fled his country in August, 1869, he found in that *pontón,* as he called Curaçao,[4] many of his old friends: the generals León Colina, Miguel Gil, and Juan Bautista García, as well as such civilians as Martín J. Sanabria and Hilario Parra. This group maintained relations with a Revolutionary Committee in Caracas, of which the following notables were members: Diego Bautista Urbaneja, and the generals Jacinto Gutiérrez and José Ramón Tello.[5]

The conspiratorial activities of these men and their personal involvement in the effort to overthrow the conservative Caracas Blues cannot be doubted. Guzmán Blanco even admitted this himself.[6] The Dutch chargé d'affaires in Caracas, Rolandus, also gave convincing evidence. On Curaçao, Antonio Leocadio Guzmán had prepared the intellectual apology for the new rebellion, a seditious pamphlet entitled *El Evangelio Liberal,* published in three parts, defending the Yellow cause.[7] These efforts were coordinated and directed by the recognized leader, Antonio Guzmán Blanco.

De Rouville still hesitated, knowing too well that today's exiles could be tomorrow's government. In several letters to the Dutch Minister for the Colonies he defended his point of view. He was joined in this protest by prominent merchants. Meanwhile the news of the expulsion order had leaked to the populace. No less than 292 inhabitants petitioned the King to stop the order.[8] The island's press pleaded in favor of the refugees, the *Civilisadó* more vehemently than the moderate *Curaçaosche Courant.* The Colonial *Raad* met in special session to discuss the expulsion and one of its vociferous members exclaimed loudly: "The illegality of that order is the more unpleasant for me because it was provoked by our Consul General in Venezuela,"[9] an exclamation illustrating the low esteem in which members of Curaçao's commercial elite held this diplomat.

The loud protests of De Rouville and the island's mercantile class only stiffened De Waal's resolve. His decision was based not solely on ignorance but also on minimal interest. The West Indian colonies formed but a tiny part of the Dutch colonial empire, which contributed no profits to the Dutch treasury, and required subsidies.

Thus, De Rouville had no choice. The axiom of political liberty was not yet applicable to a colony. Frank and free discussion of orders was beyond the governor's prerogative. The latter, realizing the fatal error his superior was about to commit, commented bitterly: "For the first time since Bolívar, people are punished by expulsion, contrary to the old established Curaçao hospitality as always applied before my term: expulsion only for those who disturb law and order in the colony." [10]

De Rouville's persistent protests and his reluctance to comply with unwise and dangerous orders sealed his fate. He was dismissed. It is probable that the intrigues of Rolandus carried some weight in the ministerial decision. During 1870 the chargé d'affaires stayed in Curaçao for some time, and it soon became obvious that he and the governor clashed on almost every topic regarding Venezuela. Consequently, De Waal accused De Rouville of "identification with the system of aggression of the party of exiled Venezuelans," [11] and replaced him in September, 1870, with the St. Martin island commissioner, Hermanus F. G. Wagner.

De Rouville's dismissal ended the first act in the development of a completely new phase in relations between Curaçao and Venezuela. This phase was dominated by the republic's new master for eighteen years, Antonio Guzmán Blanco, soon to be called the Illustrious American.

4. FIRST SKIRMISHES

Antonio Guzmán Blanco left Curaçao secretly "because of the intimidation of the colonial government," in the words of his panegyrist,
Francisco Gonzáles Guinán.[1] He embarked on a ship destined for
Martinique. But during the voyage he changed ships and an open boat
— either by arrangement or by pure coincidence — brought him to
Curamichate. Here he was well received by various leaders opposed to
the conservative Caracas rulers. With admirable vigor he began to
organize his forces, starting a successful campaign with clockwork
precision.[2] On April 27, barely ten weeks after his departure from
Curaçao, he made his glorious entry into the capital. Although a few
pockets of resistance continued a hopeless fight for some time to come,
most of the country was soon firmly under his control.

Nothing better illustrates Guzmán Blanco's success than the simultaneous happy departure of Yellow exiles from Curaçao and the gloomy
arrival of conservative fugitives from Venezuela. The latter soon became
aware of the hostility of the majority of the island population, the
Colonial *Raad,* and De Rouville toward the expulsion order, issued
under pressure of the Blue government and on the recommendation of
Rolandus. This hostility had intensified with the retaliatory actions
committed in the last days of Blue power against Dutch subjects and
shipping. Within the three-mile zone, for example, a Dutch *falouche*
(sloop) chased by the Venezuelan (Blue) war schooner *Unión* of the
expiring conservative regime, became stranded on a reef along the
Curaçao coast. While the crew had barely been able to save their skins,
the *Unión* had plundered the sloop on Dutch territory.[3] This and other
provocative actions of the now desperate conservative rulers caused
increasingly intense indignation which approached the breaking point
when Guzmán Blanco's government replaced them.

The new Yellow government did not intend to apologize for the errors
of its predecessor or to indemnify previous wrongdoings. On the contrary,
the Yellow mood soon manifested itself, adding to the mounting concern
of the Dutch governor in Willemstad.

On May 4, 1870, when Guzmán Blanco had been in the capital

exactly one week, a Dutch ship, the *Honfleur*, owned by Jesurun & Son, was seized in the port of La Guaira. The *Honfleur*, although sailing under the Dutch flag, was chartered by the former Venezuelan government to serve as a packet-boat between St. Thomas, La Guaira, Puerto Cabello, and Curaçao. In seizing the ship, Guzmán Blanco claimed to be acting within his prerogative as the legitimate successor of his defeated opponent. When Curaçao's colonial government learned of this seizure, it immediately sent another ship to La Guaira to pick up the mail. This schooner returned with additional news regarding the retaliatory policy of Venezuela's strong man: no ship could enter La Guaira's port without authorization from the new government.[4]

Rolandus, the Dutch chargé d'affaires in Caracas, immediately cried wolf, angrily protesting the seizure of the *Honfleur*. He was joined in this protest by all members of the diplomatic corps, undoubtedly because the important mail service was interrupted. After a renewed protest by Rolandus, the new government's Minister of Foreign Affairs, Antonio Leocadio Guzmán, recently arrived from Curaçao, bluntly called Rolandus "an obstacle to the good relations which Venezuela wished to maintain with the Netherlands."[5] Rolandus' reaction to this statement was rather foolish. After discussing it with some of his diplomatic corps colleagues in Caracas, but not with The Hague or its closest Dutch official, the Governor of Curaçao, he asked for his passport. It was handed to him after two days, together with another statement from Guzmán strongly expressing Venezuela's desire for good diplomatic relations with The Hague.[6] An unfortunate incident en route to La Guaira added to Rolandus' irritation: he could not produce the required permit. Several days passed, and when he finally arrived at the Venezuelan port where a Dutch man-of-war from Curaçao awaited him, his anger reached the boiling point. Guzmán, in the meantime, had informed members of the diplomatic corps by circular letter what had happened, sincerely deploring the difficulties concerning the permit.[7] At the same time, a message was dispatched to the Netherlands requesting the recall of Rolandus but emphasizing energetically the strong wish for good relations.[8] This letter was not received before the end of June.

At the end of May, the eldest partner of the Jesurun House, Abraham J. Jesurun, in his concern over the fate of the *Honfleur*, sailed on the *Sarah*, another of the firm's schooners, to La Guaira thereby ignoring the explicit orders of the Guzmán Blanco regime that La Guaira be closed. The inevitable occurred: the *Sarah* was seized by port authorities for violating the new regulation, and Jesurun was forbidden to return.

Later, the *Sarah*'s seizure and the action against Jesurun were justified by the government, which claimed that the *Sarah* had carried 1,000 rifles and other war materiel to La Guaira.[9]

The role of the Jesurun House in Venezuelan affairs calls for further elaboration. The economic might of Curaçao Jews in this period was strikingly evidenced in their financial dealings. The Jesurun firm had, since 1848, advanced huge sums to the Venezuelan government against the guarantee of bonds and the customs receipts of various ports. In 1858, regarded as the "little Rothschilds" of the Caribbean, the Jesuruns were even granted a thirty-year concession by the republic's rulers to develop a textile industry in their territory. General Falcón, later president of the country, stifled anti-Semitic feelings unleashed during the Coro disorders of 1855 [10] and in 1864 sent a delegation to Curaçao to conclude a new loan with Abraham J. Jesurun. This loan was renewed and increased in 1866.[11]

Many Jewish firms on the island owned ships during this period, and some had dockyards where they built and repaired them. Between 1843 and 1875, the Jesurun House managed a mercantile fleet of more than one hundred vessels varying in size from 25 to 275 tons.[12] Some of them had been cruising the Caribbean since the early forties, a few of them traveling as far away as New York and Amsterdam. Between 1857 and 1862 the Jesuruns owned three dockyards which built ships varying from 25 to 110 tons.[13]

The new agreement of 1866 closely connected the commercial interest of this house with the political development of Venezuela. It established as an alarming reality the fact that certain inhabitants of an island completely dependent on its trade with the instable Venezuelan republic had become highly important creditors of this selfsame republic, and vitally interested in the management of its administration.

With the seizure of the *Honfleur* and the *Sarah,* Rolandus' abrupt departure, and Jesurun's arrest, the ingredients for a serious conflict were on hand. The extremely frank Venezuelan note of May 22, asking for the recall of Rolandus, spurred the Dutch government to action.[14] By Royal Decree Werner von Bergen, interim chargé d'affaires of the North Germanic Union, was entrusted with the care of Dutch subjects and interests in Venezuela. When he left in December, his successor Von Gülick, took over.[15]

The next step was the immediate reinforcement of Dutch naval power in the Caribbean. The war frigate, *Admiraal van Wassenaar,* was sent to the West to join the one man-of-war stationed in Curaçao.

Its commander had vague instructions "to protect Dutch interests" and to await further orders.[16] The Hague did not yet understand that military pressure would only provoke anger and prove ineffective. It would learn this lesson the hard way.

With the publication of certain details of the conflict in the *Nederlandsche Staatscourant* (Dutch Official Gazette), the public and members of the States General were informed for the first time of the existing strained relations.[17] As the Cabinet was responsible to Parliament, an interpellation of the Foreign Minister was to be expected and took place on June 23. The decision of the Minister for the Colonies to expel the four Venezuelans was denounced as illegal; the course of action followed by Rolandus, who had jeopardized diplomatic relations without consulting his government, was likewise condemned.

The Dutch Foreign Minister was not very vigorous in Rolandus' defense.[18] In calling the chargé d'affaires "a good, energetic man, perhaps in some respects too honest and therefore difficult," he invited only more criticism, concern, and questioning. His denial of Rolandus' incorrect appraisal of the Venezuelan situation channelled the Chamber's anger into an open accusation that the envoy was incompetent. Had the Chamber known the folly this minister was about to commit, it would have voiced its criticism even more harshly.

New orders awaited the commander of the *Admiraal van Wassenaar* in Curaçao. As a result he and the other man-of-war, the *Kijkduin*, sailed to La Guaira requesting the return of the *Honfleur* and the *Sarah*. The Dutch warships carried with them an important passenger, Rolandus, with instructions to demand an apology.[19]

The arrival of the two Dutch men-of-war at La Guaira pressured the Venezuelan government into returning the *Honfleur* and the *Sarah* (Jesurun had already escaped) at once. However, Venezuela refused steadfastly to accept Rolandus. The Dutch chargé d'affaires thus returned to Curaçao a humiliated man. Incredible as it may seem, this slap in the face little affected the Dutch Foreign Minister. He seems to have been of the opinion, fostered by Rolandus, that the Guzmán Blanco regime was only a "temporary de facto rule," while the legitimate (Blue) government continued to reside in Maracaibo and Puerto Cabello.[20] Somewhat contradictory in this comedy of contradictions was De Waal's June 28 note to Guzmán, expressing Dutch surprise at the treatment of Rolandus and affirming the Dutch government's confidence in the chargé d'affaires. Of course, this did not help Rolandus and could not return him to his Caracas post. The note defined the seizure of the *Honfleur* as a flagrant violation of inter-national law.[21] At that time, the Dutch Foreign Minister did not yet know about the seizure of the *Sarah*.

The Venezuelan reply to this note, dated August 12, arrived in The Hague about a month later. Although reaffirming a strong desire for good relations — a constant in Guzmán's correspondence as Minister of Foreign Affairs — the note should have served as a warning to the Dutch Foreign Minister, for it was accompanied by a long memorandum and an extensive list of complaints. True to form, he did not heed the ominous signs, for if there was one prominent quality in the man who had to conduct Dutch foreign policy in those years, it was short-sightedness.

5. VENEZUELAN COMPLAINTS

The Venezuelan government quickly attacked the Dutch note of June 28, making it clear that although Rolandus was not acceptable as a representative of his country, diplomatic ties with the Netherlands were strongly desired. Guzmán claimed that proof of Rolandus' unacceptability was not necessary: if Venezuelan authorities could not work with this Dutch chargé d'affaires, then another should be sent in his place. The seizure of the *Honfleur*, it was explained, would never have grown to such dimensions had there been a more flexible man in charge of Dutch interests. If the person of Rolandus thus stood in the way of good relations between the two nations, what could be more simple than to replace him with someone acceptable to the new regime? The force of this argument, though negative, was lost on the Dutch Foreign Minister. Even the additional statement that the Venezuelan government would deplore it greatly if this incident were a cause for a suspension in relations did not rouse the Dutch Minister from his lethargy.

The lack of response and limited understanding shown by this Cabinet member are clearly shown in his note to the States General of December 1.[1] It either completely overlooked the objections against Rolandus or defined them as without foundation. It did demonstrate a certain force in arguing that it was difficult to appreciate Venezuelan desires for good relations if two Dutch men-of-war were needed to bring back the *Honfleur* and the *Sarah*.

The Venezuelan note, accompanied by a long list of complaints,[2] is a key document of nineteenth-century Dutch-Venezuelan relations. In the following discussion of this lengthy document and the replies of the Dutch Foreign Minister as given to the Second Chamber, we will use the Dutch jurist Karel H. Corporaal's framework,[3] adding some pertinent observations made by the new Governor of Curaçao.

Significantly, the first complaints concerned Guzmán Blanco's expulsion. The lack of any proof of subversive activity on his part and the degrading way in which the affair was conducted were cited. Although the legality of the expulsion was debatable in the eyes of some members of the Dutch Parliament, the Foreign Minister was able to disprove most of the Venezuelan accusations.

He fared less well with the second series of complaints, those concerning Rolandus. The Venezuelans accused the latter of having spread misinformation about their country. He was said to be a silent partner of the Jesurun House. He had not bothered to inform the Governor of Curaçao of the change in government which had occurred in Caracas on April 27, considering this only a temporary setback for the Blues. Although he refuted these grievances, the Dutch Foreign Minister could not hide the fact that strong animosity existed between the Guzmán Blanco group and the Dutch chargé d'affaires.[4]

Next came a group of complaints concerned with the slow recognition of the new regime and the continued belligerency status of the defeated Blues under General José Mariá Hernández. Even more irritating, the colonial government had discriminated against the new rulers by, for example, permitting General Adolfo A. Olivo and 130 of his men to transfer at Klein Curaçao (Little Curaçao), in Dutch territorial waters, from the Danish schooner *Dos Amigos* to the steamer *Federación* of the conservative faction, while forbidding officers of the new government sent to Curaçao to board the war schooner *27 de Abril* and sail this ship to La Guaira. The vital issue at stake here was the colonial governor's right to consider both Venezuelan contenders belligerent parties. He had already alerted the commanders of all Venezuelan ships in the Curaçao islands that they could not replenish and had to leave with the same crew with which they arrived. The *27 de Abril*, Governor Wagner observed, was free to leave, but with due regard for island regulations stipulating that a man-of-war of one belligerent party could not leave earlier than 24 hours after a man-of-war of the other party had left.[5]

A sore point in these complaints was the non-recognition of Jacob Rois Mendes, a Dutch subject and Curaçao Jew, as commercial agent of the new government. Meanwhile the former acting Attorney General, Salomon Senior, also a Dutch subject and Curaçao Jew, and sympathetic to the Blues, continued to clear ships for Coro and Maracaibo where conservatives were still strongly entrenched — Senior being their commercial representative. Since this occurred to the detriment of Guzmán Blanco's treasury, the new regime closed these ports simply by declaring them blockaded.

The Dutch Foreign Minister's militant refutation of this point did not produce a jewel of clarity. His arguments triggered an unhappy reaction among many members of the Second Chamber. Wagner spoke more clearly to the issue. The blockade of the two ports in question was not effective, he argued; it was merely a paper blockade. If the Caracas government considered its opponents' ships "pirates", this did not justify the colonial government's endorsing their definition.

Within this set of complaints, a few details demand closer attention. The colonial government, announced the Dutch Foreign Minister, was under strict orders "to act according to rules of international law in case of a civil war in Venezuela." This meant differing with the policy of the contending parties in the republic: indulgence for themselves and severity for others. The Foreign Minister also maintained that not much could be done about the *Noticioso,* a second-rate pamphlet published irregularly in Curaçao which condemned the Guzmán Blanco regime. There was freedom of the press in Curaçao as long as law and order were not endangered; one of the reasons for the expulsion of the Guzmans had been the publication of *El Evangelio Liberal.*

A fourth set of complaints centered around the contraband trade, meaning trade with the party not in power. As previously mentioned, this activity effectively contributed to the wealth of certain Curaçao families. Specific actions were enumerated. Guzmán accused these merchants, most of them involved in trade in war materiel, of delivering to his opponents 2,000 pieces of textiles (clothes and blankets) and of concluding loans up to U.S. $ 30,000, covered by custom-duty receipts from Maracaibo and serving as payment for all kinds of commodities sold to these opponents. Coal was repeatedly transferred, he claimed, from Dutch schooners to "pirate-steamers," as Blue ships were called. The Blue *Marapari,* for instance, had taken on coal in the port of Curaçao.

Regulations regarding export of war materiel, the complaints continued, were poorly enforced and regularly dodged. In addition, they were prejudicial to the new regime. The Venezuelan Minister noted, for example, that the *Amalia* (owned by the Jesurun House) had departed from Curaçao on July 5 destined for Santo Domingo, but part of its cargo was transferred on the high seas to another ship and the rest in Santo Domingo to the Dutch schooner *Carolina* (property of the Dutch subject, Isaac Haim Pereira, a Jewish merchant of Curaçao). In both cases, the cargo had reached the port of Coro and the Blues.

As Corporaal rightly observes,[6] the problem stemmed from the loopholes in the island's regulation of 1858 regarding the export of war materiel and the inability or unwillingness of the colonial government to enforce it satisfactorily. Indeed, war materiel left the Curaçao port regularly for Santo Domingo and Haiti, where captains then received a certificate that it was not unloaded in a revolutionary section of the country. From there it was sent to Venezuela. Sometimes it was even directly transported from Curaçao with certification purchased elsewhere. The colonial government tried to stop this practice in vain by requiring that unloading take place in the presence of a Dutch consul. Merchants were adept at finding ports where there was no Dutch consul.

The Dutch Foreign Minister's refutation was unclear and far from strong. Determinedly loyal to the sacred gospel of free trade — as was the Governor of Curaçao — he hotly defended it in spite of flagrant transgressions. No government, he argued, could be required to place obstacles in the way of free trade and commerce in its territory for the sake of another government. It would be preposterous to ask colonial authorities to do so. If President Guzmán Blanco objected, he should try to stop this trade himself. Ships were permitted in port for repairs and coal. Even "pirates" were given this treatment in neutral ports. What happened outside of Curaçao's territorial waters was not the responsibility of the colonial government.

The complaint that the Dutch man-of-war *Kijkduin* convoyed three Dutch ships to Coro, one of the ports blockaded by the Guzmán regime, under the pretext of bringing back Dutch subjects while in reality merchandise was brought to Curaçao was, the Dutch Foreign Minister emphasized, an insinuation, adding that a Dutch man-of-war was free to do convoy duty. Despite an ensuing hot debate — the Chamber did not swallow this nonsense — he refused to give interpellating members further particulars on this matter. Governor Wagner's correspondence makes clear that Dutch subjects had indeed been brought back by the *Kijkduin* and that the so-called merchandise was part of their property.

Last but not least came the grievances against the Jesurun House, including reasons for the seizure of the *Honfleur* and the *Sarah*. Jesurun himself was considered by the new rulers — and probably rightly so — as the chief supplier of war materiel to the opponents of the *guzmancista* government. This government considered him their agent; he traveled around making propaganda against the new regime to obtain support for the Blues. He conducted himself as minister plenipotentiary, concluded contracts, participated in councils, and used his wealth and ships to fight the Yellows. He had even been so brazen as to come to La Guaira where the new government could have rightly imprisoned him. Out of respect for his nationality, it had only prohibited his leaving the republic unless he foreswore further interference in Venezuelan internal affairs. This he had stubbornly refused to do because the new government had not recognized his claims. A pledge of non-interference by Jesurun to the Governor of Curaçao might have solved many problems, it was suggested. The governor, however, had not reacted. In the meantime, Jesurun had gone into hiding and sailed back to Curaçao aboard the *Eduardo* under Italian flag.

The *Honfleur,* continued the Venezuelan document, was no Dutch packet-boat, but rather a Dutch ship chartered by the Venezuelan government to transport mail. The diplomatic corps, concerned about its seizure, had protested because of misinformation provided by Rolandus; consequently, it had not joined him in his second protest. The *Sarah* was seized because it had brought 1,000 rifles and other war materiel to La Guaira while that port was still in the hands of the Blues. On orders of the former regime the *Sarah* had sailed to Maturín, and on its way back to La Guaira this port had changed hands.

The Dutch Foreign Minister stressed in his answer that any transaction with the conservative regime — as long as it had some power — could not be considered a violation of neutrality. If Jesurun had committed a crime against the Venezuelan government — the new one — it should have arrested and tried him. It had not done so. With regard to the claims of his firm against that government, the Minister did not consider them his government's concern. Conveniently, the issue of Jesurun's loans was omitted together with its possible political implication and the fact that even Rolandus once had warned about the consequences and the possibility of an inflation of Jesurun's claims.

In retrospect, Jesurun's conduct is not too difficult to assess. His firm had committed itself with loan after loan to successive liberal Venezuelan governments and not one of them had been able to maintain itself in power, let alone honor its financial commitments. As soon as conservatives obtained control of the administration and Jesurun's hopes of repayment dimmed, the Curaçao firm sustained the exiled Yellows, providing them with arms and long-term credit in another bid for power. In this operation, the Jesurun fleet was placed at the disposal of the liberals and transported their troops and provisions. All this was proffered for usurious prices as the risk was high. Consequently, if these efforts produced the desired results and the liberals gained control, they would be faced with a costly bill for services, materiel, loans, and damages incurred in support of their cause.[7]

If they refused to pay, Jesurun, in a shrewd analysis of the situation, could choose among several alternatives. He could change parties and start the same game again with the Blues. If neither of the two parties was willing to pay he could demand The Hague's diplomatic support which, foolishly enough, was always given. This sometimes produced results, although in that case the role of the Dutch envoy in Caracas was not an enviable one. This explains, at least partly, Guzmán Blanco's rage against Rolandus. His feelings toward the Dutch representative never changed, but his attitude toward Jesurun did. The compounded problems of the Venezuelan treasury, dramatically increased by Venezuelan political instability, forced the new aggressive ruler to view Jesurun's wealth and credit as vital to his nation's survival.[8]

Shortly after the Dutch Foreign Minister had answered the hectic interpellation of the Second Chamber — "very unsatisfactorily" as a special committee later observed — one of the regular shufflings in the Dutch Cabinets of those days caused his replacement by Baron Gericke van Herwijnen, a somewhat more conservative member of the Dutch ruling elite. Changes in Venezuela were more spectacular, as they resulted in Guzmán Blanco's virtual control of the republic. Consequently, the seizure of Dutch ships trading with his opponents decreased as there were fewer ports through which to disembark arms and ammunition for the Blues. A main source of irritation and persistent concern was thus eliminated.[9] Some incidents continued to occur, of course, and clouded the promise of a brighter future.[10]

In this unfolding small-scale Caribbean drama, the attitude of the Curaçao governor perfectly reflected that of his liberal-minded superiors in The Hague. During the latter half of the nineteenth century, the Kingdom of the Netherlands was ruled by liberal Cabinets. Although they alternated — as in Great Britain — with more conservative-oriented ministries, the general tag of liberalism, extreme or moderate, can safely be applied to all of them. Free trade was the gospel of the period. That this atttitude would involve the Dutch in a fray with the Venezuelan republic was regarded as a minor risk.

Nevertheless, at this point The Hague was willing to bargain, knowing that further causes of friction with the republic had to be eliminated. It arranged a compromise in the form of a Royal Decree which would replace — at the Curaçao governor's convenience — the loosely written colonial regulation of 1858 regarding the trade in war materiel. Dated

February 27, 1871, the Royal Decree prohibited all export from Curaçao of firearms, gunpowder, and other war materiel, with violation punishable by imprisonment and/or fine.[11] In case of seizure and arrest, the confiscation of cargo and ship could follow.[12]

This decree inherently conceded greater independence to the Governor of Curaçao. It became his prerogative to enforce or to suspend the decree, depending on his judgment and the advice of the Colonial *Raad*. If the governor suspended it — and he was also required to consult the chargé d'affaires in Caracas, hopefully soon to be appointed — the regulation of 1858 would once again go into effect.

This Royal Decree, intended to last one year, was received in the colony by the end of March and became effective April 8. Wagner's speed is understandable since the export of war materiel greatly endangered already strained relations with Venezuela.[13]

If The Hague now expected a period of relaxation, it greatly underestimated the smugglers' wits and ingenuity. Clouds again accumulated over the blue skies of Curaçao and a multitude of incidents soured the life of its governor. Guzmán Blanco, completing his victorious control over the Venezuelan republic, viewed the island as a major factor compounding his existing problems. His opponents, determined to end the Great Liberal's rule as quickly as possible, opened new roads toward that goal during their Curaçao exile, conspiring in their usually noisy way and launching campaigns for funds and loans to which greedy merchants were willing to succumb.

In late November, 1870, the Attorney General of the Curaçao colony, Willem Sassen, suggested that the governor evict the American schooner *Virginius,* suspected of piracy.[14] Wagner did not heed this advice, perhaps because of the mounting animosity between himself and the Attorney General, the highest ranking colonial official under his jurisdiction. Sassen ebulliently maintained that the *Virginius* had chased the Dutch schooner *Ofir* as "a pirate of the worst kind." [15] What really happened illustrates the unfortunate and complicated nature of the problems racking the island and the republic.

The *Ofir* (owner unknown) had left Curaçao destined for St. Martin. Outside the island's territorial waters it had delivered coal and provisions to a Blue flotilla. The *Virginius* had also left Curaçao destined for Cuba, where the Ten Years' War promised unlimited profits for unscrupulous traders, but, for some reason, had changed course and joined the naval forces of Guzmán Blanco off Puerto Cabello, seizing his opponents' schooners and trying vainly to capture the *Ofir*.[16] On

December 8, the *Virginius,* which had dropped anchor again in Curaçao, left of its own free will, thus relieving the governor of at least one headache. But Wagner was soon troubled by others.

Jacob Rois Mendes, who claimed to be the legitimate commercial agent of the new Venezuelan government, unleashed a series of documented complaints against the freshly-arrived exiles — now of the Blue party — who, as he maintained, were conspiring against his government by printing seditious pamphlets. Mendes was, like Jesurun, a wealthy and prominent member of the island's Jewish community, an owner of ships and a dockyard.[17] The reason for his joining the Yellows was, perhaps, simply profit.

Among the new exiles in Curaçao, General Ignacio Galán played an important role. Expel him, suggested Mendes;[18] but it was not that easy. General Hernández, who was defending the last Blue bastions in the republic, sent Wagner a letter in which he accused several Curaçao inhabitants of supporting Guzmán Blanco. Clumsily worded, the accusation lacked perspective but, shortly afterwards, Hernández fled his own country and arrived on the island to join the exiled opponents of the new ruler and to compound Wagner's problems.

Considered more closely, Mendes' complaints also included Abraham M. Chumaceiro, a Jewish lawyer who, in early 1871, published and distributed an anti-Guzmán Blanco pamphlet entitled *What in Venezuela Is Called the Liberal Party Judged by Itself* (Lo que en Venezuela llaman Partido Liberal juzgado por si mismo). In suing Chumaceiro for this attack on the new Venezuelan government, Mendes had the satisfaction of achieving a certain success. First, a Jewish judge in charge of the case, Sol Cohen Henriques, petitioned the governor to be disqualified for fear of causing unpleasant repercussions within the Jewish community. He was replaced by a Protestant. Chumaceiro then was fined 200 guilders plus 50 guilders in court costs.[19]

The main thrust of Mendes' complaints had no effect. No Venezuelans were expelled. As Wagner pointed out to the commercial agent, there was no written proof of conspiracy. Besides, the Curaçao governor at this point seemed almost obsessed by an exquisite consciousness of neutrality with regard to the belligerents in Venezuela.

Shortly before the end of 1870, the Dutch schooner *La Gracia de Dios,* unaware that Coro had changed hands, was seized by the *guzmancista* officials of that town. The ship was the property of Jeudah Senior, a Curaçao Jew and sympathizer of the Blues. He immediately requested colonial intervention on his behalf.[20] Wagner, deeply concerned, considered the request to be reasonable. The commander of the man-of-war stationed in Curaçao (*Amstel*) received orders to investigate this seizure and, if necessary, demand restitution. At the same time, he had orders to avoid violence.[21] The *Amstel* left Curaçao January 10 and returned a week later with the news that the new regime had incorporated the ship into its embryonic war navy. There was no real effort to obtain the release of the schooner. But at the end of March, Wagner received the news from Guzmán that his government, to show its good faith, had ordered the return of the seized ship.[22]

The central problem faced by Wagner was how to interpret the new regime's actions in this and other cases and how to discern some coherence in apparently whimsical acts. The generous gesture seems to have been part of an elaborate campaign initiated by Guzmán to pressure the colonial government into certain actions. Venezuelan dependence on Caribbean islands like Curaçao and Trinidad for its imports and exports irritated the Great Liberal and his father and offended growing national pride in the republic. Added to this situation — already an intolerable one for Guzmán Blanco — was the vast extent of illegal trade which hurt the Venezuelan treasury considerably.

Realization of this particular Venezuelan attitude grew slowly, for at this date the new regime's actions were hardly coherent. Guzmán had not yet clearly defined his goals and was still groping in the dark. But it is evident that he was aware of Curaçao's stranglehold over the Venezuelan economy and tried to reverse that situation. Still probing his course, his actions confused and mystified the cool and unimpulsive Wagner.

At the beginning of February, 1871, the Curaçao governor was approached by José María Ortega —a general of considerable reputation in the new regime — commissioned to negotiate for the return of two Venezuelan men-of-war at anchor in the Curaçao port which had served the conservative cause before its collapse.[23] Somewhat earlier, Mendes had sent the governor a letter regarding the two vessels.[24] But Guzmán's special representative raised the topic to such a level that Wagner could no longer ignore it. Calling Guzmán's approach "a bombastic introduction" — Wagner never understood the Illustrious American's mind — the Curaçao governor was confronted with a firm demand: return the ships.[25] Guzmán tried to bolster this request by implying that fighting in Venezuela had ended and that a belligerent Blue faction no longer existed. The Dutch governor considered this wishful thinking and denied the request.

Perhaps it would have been wiser if Wagner had acceded, since

Guzmán's ingenuity in pursuing his goals could hardly be called wavering. Instead of again making the same request, he introduced a set of new complaints adding them to the Venezuelan litany of August 12, 1870. Now, however, the tone was definitely bitter.[26] In order to obtain maximum result, their strategic aspects were now inflated with the slighting remark that

> "the policy which is developing systematically could result in a palpably bellicose situation, but will be incapable of materializing the goal of an assault on Venezuela, whose twenty states now are united under the Federal Government. It is, however, capable of causing disturbances in part of the Western coast, to burden our treasury, to keep the torch of dissent burning, and to cause the shedding of more and more Venezuelan blood." [27]

Other vessels (under Venezuelan or Dutch flag), he wrote, leave Curaçao with rebels aboard to execute expeditions against our country. His pent-up rage exploded with a threat: "We will immediately order that all communication of whatever character or under whatever flag be broken." He realized that this could cost "sensitive losses to the innocent people of Curaçao" and "witness a long series of hostilities." [28]

Wagner remained cool in spite of these hot words. He wrote his superior, the Dutch Minister for the Colonies, of the attempts of the Venezuelan dictator to pressure him, and outlined what he had done to prevent further Venezuelan complaints.[29] Rejecting as ridiculous the rumors of a planned attack on the island, he referred to a sore point of Venezuelan anger: exiled Blues on colonial soil. In recognizing this irritation, he felt that it could not be removed by regulation or prohibition within the liberal framework of certain freedoms. In addition, geographical proximity of the island would remain as an insurmountable obstacle to efforts to end tensions. Modestly phrasing his conclusions, he wrote: "I agree with Mr. Guzmán that this exercises a certain influence on affairs of his country." But that Guzmán Blanco could tilt the tables by seizing the island the governor rejected. He had a low regard for the Venezuelan fleet: "it would be scattered," he growled, "by the *Amstel* alone." [30]

These complaints demonstrated the other side's careful watch over the island, aided by efficient spying. Understandably reluctant, Wagner was forced to accept the revealing evidence of a division in the Curaçao population between Blues and Yellows.[31] Nor did matters improve with the publication of the acrimonious comments of the Guzmán Blanco regime's well-known mouthpiece, the vociferous *Opinión Nacional,* a paper which helped foster a pronounced anti-Dutch sentiment in the republic.

There were more complications. Before Guzmán Blanco's rise to power in 1870, the conservative government had seized three Dutch schooners owned by Curaçao Jews, among them the *Adelicia,* belonging to Mendes. The Yellow regime returned them promptly because the owners were all sympathizers and supporters of the liberal cause, and at least one was compensated for damages.[32]

Most incidents, however, incurred discomfort and tension for the colonial government, and conditions in the course of 1871 became increasingly explosive. In May, 1871, Wagner received a letter from General Venancio Pulgar, accusing the owner of the plantation Piscadera on Curaçao of manufacturing firearms and cartridges for the Blues.[33] In September, the bark *Gobernador de Aruba,* filled with arms and ammunition, stranded on a Curaçao reef and broke in two.[34]

Thus, as the year 1871 rapidly passed, the battle lines became more firmly drawn. War materiel continued to be exported in spite of the Royal Decree, and the colonial government — often accused of being in league with the merchants — struggled desperately to adopt the correct neutral position. The governor, it seems, could not always count upon the full cooperation of higher colonial officials. This probably occurred in the case of General Matías Salazar, who in October had published in Curaçao a manifesto arousing the Great Liberal's wrath because it announced his future destruction. Before Wagner could interfere, the general had fled. The Venezuelan government was properly informed of this.[35]

In February, 1872, Wagner extended the Royal Decree.[36] The effects of this policy slowly grew more apparent with each passing month and in the long run seem to have kept exports well under control. At the same time, Guzmán Blanco's grasp on the Venezuelan republic also grew stronger. Although moderation and dignity did not always characterize his regime's dealing with its opponents, a relaxation of tensions resulted and self-restraint was applied to its observance of peaceful conservatives.

Yet Wagner's good expectations were newly challenged. Some Curaçao merchants, faced with the end of the profitable trade in arms and war materiel, grew restless. They first requested the governor suspend the new decree, which was within his prerogatives. After meeting with surly refusal, they asked that Rolandus, still on the island, take their request to the Foreign Office in The Hague.[37] Foolishly enough, the former chargé d'affaires consented. The petition was denied.[38]

Now the relations between Curaçao and the republic moved rapidly toward a more favorable latitude. In June, 1872, Wagner suggested a suspension of the Royal Decree on condition that Venezuela did not object,[39] and made himself an instant friend of all war materiel merchants. The Hague, however, objected, and advocated a more cautious course, fearing that the island would once again become a center of conspiracy and smuggling against the Caracas government. The happy softening of tensions seemed to promise long duration when, in the fall, a new Dutch chargé d'affaires arrived in the Venezuelan capital to replace the unlucky Rolandus.

6. RESTORATION OF RELATIONS

In spite of continuous Venezuelan complaints about export of war materiel, the colonial government's attitude toward (Blue) exiles, the seizure of Dutch ships, and other irritating actions, the severed diplomatic relations worried Guzmán Blanco, and he repeatedly assured Wagner of his regime's friendly dispostion.[1] By late 1870, the Venezuelan Foreign Minister had begun to ponder the best solution to this problem. In nominating J. M. Torres Caicedo as ambassador to The Hague, he chose an experienced diplomat who was categorized as a staunch liberal and had performed well in an earlier conflict during the Falcón presidency. Torres was in Paris, however, which was under siege by the Prussian army.[2] Eager to end the impasse, Guzmán now turned to the Venezuelan ambassador in France, Lucio Pulido, who at that time happened to be in Liège (Luik), Belgium, for health reasons. On April 18, 1871, this representative of the Venezuelan government arrived in The Hague and requested an audience with the Dutch Foreign Minister, Baron L. Gericke van Herwijnen.[3]

Like Torres, Pulido was a loyal follower of the Great Liberal Party, and together with his brother, General José Ignacio Pulido, was well-known among the new ruling elite. In spite of Pulido's astute maneuvering it took a year before a new Dutch chargé d'affaires was accepted by Caracas.[4]

The Dutch Foreign Minister appreciated the Venezuelan approach and was quite willing to abandon what seemed to be the main obstacle to improved rapport: Rolandus. Given the Dutch willingness to sacrifice their former representative, both countries suddenly found a basis on which they could conduct negotiations. There was no effort to have Rolandus accepted temporarily to save Dutch face "because of the invincible repugnance" of the Guzmán Blanco regime.[5]

Two aspects of the incident still remained to be settled. The first had a double objective: an official apology demanded by the Dutch, ostensibly the offended party, in which the Venezuelan government would express its regret for what had happened and declare its sincere desire to reestablish durable ties. This would manifest itself in the reception of a new Dutch representative in Caracas with "exceptional honors." [6] The second point was more complicated, having to do with claims of Dutch subjects in Curaçao against the Venezuelan government. Without recognizing the full amount of these claims, Pulido astutely suggested postponing discussions on this topic until after renewal of normal diplomatic relations. The Dutch Foreign Minister acceded, thereby suffering severe criticism in the Second Chamber. He defended himself by observing that agreement on these claims would be difficult to negotiate without normal diplomatic contact.[7]

Crucial to the comprehension of this incident is the fact that both countries were willing to assume certain responsibilities in order to arrive at a durable mutual understanding. Pulido and Gericke van Herwijnen signed the definite protocol on March 21, 1872, and six days later Pulido was received by King William III. The Venezuelan envoy expressed his government's sincere regret at the disruption and its honest desire to enjoy satisfactory, long-lasting relations. The constitutional monarch replied with platitudes of appreciation and high expectations for the future, his speech having been prepared by the Dutch Cabinet.[8] Two days later, both countries issued a joint declaration which deferred financial claims to "later negotiations" in Caracas. There, claims would be examined and discussed with the new Dutch chargé d'affaires.[9]

In view of subsequent events, these negotiations are interesting. Their results reflected the slow recognition of the real cause of friction: the Dutch liberal gospel of free trade, including traffic in war materiel, and of a free press, permitting Venezuelan refugees to publish pamphlets and articles of an offensive and vindictive nature against the Caracas government. Such considerations did not enter into the debates at this time. Much attention was given instead to the Dutch King's ceremonial reception of the Venezuelan ambassador in his Royal Palace and to a similar performance in the Casa Amarilla where Guzmán Blanco would play host to the new Dutch envoy.

The Dutch and the Venezuelan press rivalled each other in proclaiming the agreement an unparalleled success for their respective nations. With the advantage of hindsight it is not difficult to determine which country achieved a victory. Venezuela, although officially cast in an apologetic role, had managed to move the crucial negotiations on Dutch claims out of The Hague, where they would have been assured of maximum support and official Dutch pressure, to Caracas where Dutch interests would not be similarly protected. The Second Chamber critics had realized this. The Dutch Foreign Minister was slow to recognize the importance of this gain for Caracas.

It now remained for the Dutch Foreign Minister to find the right man for the difficult position of chargé d'affaires. He selected Johannes Brakel, a Captain of Infantry, whose official title was "general consul and chargé d'affaires in the Republics of Venezuela, Colombia, and Ecuador." [10] As he had no previous diplomatic experience and spoke no Spanish, it is unknown what qualifications brought this soldier into the diplomatic field. This appointment meant the end of Von Gülick's term as acting representative in Caracas. He was awarded with a knighthood in the Order of the Dutch Lion.

In assuming the responsibilities of his new position, Brakel received broad instructions indicative of the Dutch view on what came to be called the "Venezuelan Question". He was required first to go to Curaçao, where he was to see Governor Wagner and Rolandus and to make an exhaustive survey of the Curaçao merchants' monetary claims by contacting them personally. His primary goal in Venezuela was to promote friendly relations, to report regularly on the financial and internal situation, to become acquainted with the authorities in Caracas, to establish good contact with members of the Diplomatic Corps, to remain aloof from internal affairs, to settle disputes orally as often as possible, and to follow strictly the orders of the Foreign Minister in The Hague. It was also recommended that special attention be paid to the claims of the Curaçao merchants.[11]

Brakel arrived in Curaçao on August 20, 1872, too late to meet Rolandus, who had left the island six weeks earlier.[12] He met Wagner several times but seems to have rejected, from the beginning, the latter's somewhat conservative views of the problem. Through an advertisement in the *Curaçaosche Courant* the island's claimants were informed of Brakel's readiness to review their respective claims against Venezuela. Several merchants made use of this offer, among them the other partner of the Jesurun House, Jacob A. Jesurun, and Jeudah Senior with his son.[13] Together with Isaac Pardo who lived in Caracas, the Seniors and the Jesuruns were the Dutch claimants to the so-called "diplomatic debts" of Venezuela. Brakel's stay on the island lasted three weeks.

On September 9, the new Dutch envoy left Willemstad on the man-of-war *Kijkduin* for La Guaira. Two days later, he had his first audience with Venezuelan Foreign Minister Guzmán in Caracas.[14] After a short discussion of the meaning of certain paragraphs of the agreement concluded with Pulido in The Hague, it was agreed that Brakel could present his credentials to the Venezuelan president. Thus, relations were restored.[15]

7. DUTCH CLAIMS

The diplomatic clash between the European and the Caribbean nation had not made the respective parties lose sight of a most urgent aspect still to be settled: that of Dutch monetary claims. Venezuela was constantly in need of money. Indeed, the Curaçao money lenders had made loans to successive governments of the republic since the days of Gran Colombia, when Curaçao Jews were invited to settle in Coro, where they were guaranteed protection and religious freedom. Around 1830, the city even seems to have had a Jewish mayor, and Jews of Curaçao origin soon constituted a vital part of the Venezuelan coastal economy.[1]

During subsequent revolutions these Jews usually cooperated closely with local governments. Understandable differences arose, however, and in 1848 some Jews complained to the Dutch consul in Coro that government purchases had remained unpaid. This was the modest beginning of a series of Dutch claims which lasted until the days of Juan Vicente Gómez, sometimes reaching explosive dimensions.

In reviewing the origin of these claims, it becomes clear that Jews were forced to cooperate with local authorities because they needed their protection. Thus the governor and the Coro military commander customarily compelled the Jews to "lend" large sums for maintaining the Coro garrison — a fort with about 300 men — and sometimes for paying government salaries. This was obviously only a small step away from pure blackmail, but the Jews were in no position to object. In 1854, however, they refused a new payment or "loan", since recent decisions in Caracas made the central government loath to back these "loans". The lack of federal guarantees stifled what little willingness the Jews felt to provide "loans".

The predictable consequence of this attitude was the disbanding of the Coro garrison under the pretext that there was no money, giving unruly elements in the population a free hand. The immediate result was the sudden circulation — perhaps supported by angry local authorities — of several pamphlets inciting the populace against the now unprotected Jews. On the night of February 4, 1855, the shops of two Dutch subjects, Jeudah Senior and Samuel L. Maduro, were plundered and several Jews mistreated. The colonial government of Curaçao, when informed of these riots, sent two men-of-war, soon to be joined by a third from the Netherlands. A general exodus of Jews from Coro to Curaçao exemplified their feelings. The refugees, 160 in all, found the entire island community in sympathy with them.[3]

This aggressive, anti-Jewish attitude was incidental and did not spread to other parts of the republic. A special Dutch envoy sent to Caracas to demand an explanation and indemnities for damages suffered was well received. Although Venezuelan authorities at first tried to draw a line between Christian and Jewish claimants, the Dutch envoy did not accept such discrimination: "We do not recognize a difference between Christian and Jew. A Dutch subject is a Dutch subject." Prolonged negotiations finally resulted in an agreement to pay victims an indemnity of 200,000 guilders (100,000 pesos).[4] Interestingly, this sum was fully paid by the year 1863, in spite of the unstable political situation of a republic in the throes of a five-year civil war.[5] In 1858, some of the affected Jews returned to Coro.

Since 1848 the house of Jesurun (constantly called Jesurum in Venezuelan documents) had been involved in certain loans to the federal government, backed by guarantees of customs receipts from various Venezuelan ports. General Falcón suppressed his strong anti-Semitic feelings, unleashed during the Coro disorders, and sent a delegation to Curaçao in 1864 to negotiate another loan with the Jesurun House.[6] After 1864, this Jewish firm became the principal Dutch money lender to the Venezuelan government. In its agreement with Falcón of 1865, 25 per cent of Maracaibo's customs-duty receipts was given as a guarantee.

The existing political confusion made new and increased loans a dire necessity.[7] In 1866 the Curaçao firm, in spite of the totally inadequate administration of public funds, committed itself to daily loan payments of 5,000 pesos (10,000 guilders) over a period of eight months, totalling 1,200,000 pesos. The Jewish house certainly accepted a risky undertaking, although from this sum would be deducted a daily amount of 1,000 pesos over the eight-month period as payment on the 1865 loan on which the Venezuelan government had not yet paid a penny. For the 1866 loan, the government offered a guarantee of 52½ per cent of the customs duties from Maracaibo and Ciudad Bolívar.[8] In addition, the firm would receive 1¼ per cent monthly interest, or 15 per cent yearly. The above-mentioned customs-duty revenues would continue as a guarantee until complete redemption. Moreover, Jesurun was to give an advance loan of 134,000 pesos, 24,000 in cash, 32,000 in bonds payable within 60 days, 32,000 within 90 days, and 46,000 within 120 days. These also bore a 1¼ per cent monthly interest rate, while 10 per cent of all incoming duties were pledged to redeem these sums. The guarantees proved to be empty; Guzmán Blanco was not the man to honor costly pledges if his interests were affected.

A dangerous aspect of these loans, unperceived at the time, was that through these transactions the financial interests of the Dutch/Jewish commercial house became closely allied with the course of Venezuelan events.[9] The two other money lenders, Jeudah Senior and Isaac Pardo, followed suit although to a much lesser extent.[10]

About the same time similar speculation involved a huge British loan, and one wonders if the Jesuruns were aware of it. In 1864, Guzmán Blanco concluded a loan in London of £ 1,500,000 or 9,750,000 *pesos,* taking for himself a whopping 5 per cent commission. This loan was also guaranteed by port duties,[11] and what customs revenues were left to run the government remain a mystery. French, Italian, Spanish, and North American speculators would also soon wonder what would happen to their carelessly invested money.

Thus a few inhabitants of an island whose economy depended on trade with Venezuela became important creditors of that republic and consequently intensely concerned with Venezuelan internal affairs. Perhaps it would have worked with a stable administration in Venezuela, a quality most nineteenth-century Venezuelan governments unfortunately lacked. As soon as the Falcón regime acquired an appearance of stability, various foreign powers with subject creditors took steps to intervene for them officially. In February 1864, for example, France concluded such an arrangement, followed by Spain in April, 1865; Denmark in March, 1866; the United States in April of that same year; and Great Britain and Italy in September and October, 1868, respectively.[12] By refusing to submit claims to arbitration and by contravening the Calvo Doctrine, which required foreign licenses to pledge in advance not to appeal to their governments for protection of their claims, these agreements adopted the principle of intervention into the internal affairs of another nation.

Because of these negotiations the debts came to be called "diplomatic debts". They included foreign claims based on damages incurred in civil war or by unjustified government actions in times of stress. The character and amount of these claims were usually established after diplomatic negotiations and were recognized by Venezuela and the foreign governments as justifiable.[13]

In 1868, the resulting political and financial imbroglio moved the Monagas regime to consolidate the agreements into one single obligation. This effort to simplify the bureaucratic side of loan payments concurred with the sincere desire to protect foreign as well as Venezuelan interests. It was misinterpreted because of the simultaneous attempts to decrease the amount of duties pledged to redeem these debts. France, which was collecting 17 per cent of the incoming duties of the customs houses of La Guaira and Puerto Cabello, frustrated this effort.[14] During the peak of these disputes, the Dutch chargé d'affaires Rolandus tried unsuccessfully to unite Great Britain, Denmark, the United States, and the Netherlands against the Caracas government, thus earning him the outspoken dislike of Guzmán Blanco.[15]

Under the combined pressure from Germany, Great Britain, Spain, Italy, and Denmark, the Guzmán Blanco regime reoffered some of Monagas' proposals.[16] The newly-formed German Empire had even sent a small squadron to demonstrate her serious intention to protect her subjects' interests.[17]

In spite of strained relations between The Hague and Caracas, or perhaps because of them, the Netherlands refused an invitation to join other protesting powers. But her complaints were the same: long overdue payment of debts. Different action for similar reasons was followed by U.S. President Grant. His somewhat reckless schemes for the expansion and extension of U.S. interests into certain areas of Latin America were soon very apparent. In his speech to Congress on December 4, 1871, he urged that body to begin action under the award of the Venezuelan Claims Commission of 1866. The president said with a touch of sarcasm: "The internal dissensions of the Venezuelan government present no justification for the absence of any effort to meet its solemn treaty obligations."

Guzmán Blanco reacted to this rather belligerent speech through his gifted mouthpiece, Foreign Minister Guzmán, who protested no less belligerently.[18] According to a letter from the Dutch ambassador in Washington, it even appears that as a result Grant advocated a punitive expedition against Venezuela,[19] although he refused to cooperate with the European powers. It certainly was not in accord with the Monroe Doctrine for the U.S. to join Europe in any action, political or otherwise, in the American hemisphere, which the U.S. wanted to draw totally into her own economic and political orbit. Nor did the German squadron accomplish anything but induce Guzmán Blanco to declare his willingness to reopen the matter which was probably the German government's goal. The U.S. offered to mediate in the impending problems of foreign claims (including her own) and thus to play the role of peacemaker. This anticipated the international policeman role Theodore Roosevelt was to proclaim in a later age.[20]

As previously mentioned, the Netherlands refused all invitations to diplomatic cooperation. Nor did she accept the suggestion of solving problems by force, believing that peaceful wooing would achieve better results. In addition, she had just agreed to discuss her claims through the newly-appointed chargé d'affaires. To a cautious Dutch government it appeared inappropriate to participate in a combined action at the moment relations were beginning to improve.

There was still another important reason for Dutch forbearance. After an almost twenty-year occupation by France (1795-1813) and a fifteen year period as a buffer-state created by the Congress of Vienna (1815-1830), the Dutch and the Belgians had adopted their separate ways. The former assumed a passive role in the European concert of nations, a role dictated by their decreasing importance in international politics. They successfully maintained this posture throughout the nineteenth century and were hesitant to compromise themselves in an alliance with the three strongest European powers: France, Germany, and Great Britain. There was no inducement for the Dutch to cooperate with any one of them. It is true that after the separation of Belgium and the development of the Dutch East India Empire, the Dutch merchant marine increased considerably and investments abroad grew rapidly. Yet the old overseas consciousness was gone forever. The Netherlands withdrew permanently from the Great Power politics in which she had dabbled for two centuries and placed great reliance on neutral status. With this policy she felt secure, and in the course of time it came to be regarded as a positive good and a sacred international duty.

The unfolding picture of new negotiations between Dutch envoy Brakel and Venezuelan Foreign Minister Guzmán changed suddenly when the latter resigned, together with the Ministers of Justice and the Interior, to participate in the coming elections. This change in the top echelon of the Venezuelan bureaucracy was interpreted by Brakel as well as by William Pile, the U.S. minister, as an unfavorable omen.[21] Brakel gained the impression after a visit to Pile that the latter intended (whether on orders from Washington or not) to push the Venezuelans into accepting a U.S. remedy to cure the foreign claims sickness.[22]

Assuring the Diplomatic Corps that retirement of the "diplomatic debts" would be arranged in reciprocal cooperation with the creditors, i.e. envoys of the foreign nations involved, the Guzmán Blanco government proposed the following:

Treasury income stemming mainly from customs duties, the major source of revenue, was assessed, for the first half of the year 1873 at 1,200,000 *pesos* or *venezolanos* (2,400,000 guilders). Of every 100 *venezolanos,* 55 would be destined for regular government expenses, and 5 for supplementary expenses. Of the remaining 40 the following arrangement was suggested:

> 27 per cent for retiring the internal debt
> 27 per cent for retiring the external debt
> 33 per cent for education and public works
> 13 per cent for "diplomatic debts" [23]

This proposal meant that for the first six months of 1873, payments destined to retire "diplomatic debts" would amount to 62,400 *venezolanos,* i.e., 5,2 per cent of the total government revenues.

Acute observers of the emerging picture soon became aware of the paradoxical use of the term "reciprocity" by the Guzmán Blanco regime. No discussion was held which indicated any concern for the views of the claimants. The latter were informed — without any accompanying letter of explanation — by sending them the *Gaceta Oficial.*[24] In the political jargon of the Venezuelan government, "proposals" meant the decisions of Guzmán Blanco. The Illustrious American was a man who had little use for discussions.

How much these Venezuelan "proposals" were influenced by the suggestions of the U.S. envoy Pile is difficult to guess.[25] Pile, whose role in these negotiations did not anticipate his peculiar and adventurous career of later days, suggested a sliding scale in which payments on the "diplomatic debts" would gradually increase. Viewing a promising foreign market, however, the U.S. cooperated far beyond merely suggesting a new scale. Moving smoothly, in Pile's plan, from benevolent paternalism to barely hidden imperialism, she promised the delivery — for payment — of rigged cutters to guard the Venezuelan coast and to curb smuggling. Although these cutters, manned by U.S. crews, would sail under the Venezuelan flag, the sisterly control was unmistakable. The second suggestion revealed an even more intensified supervision: Each Venezuelan port would station a U.S. customs officer to receive the revenue destined to pay the "diplomatic debts".[26]

The mushrooming growth of the U.S. foreign market marked her increased interest in the Latin American hemisphere. As Secretary of State, James G. Blaine formulated this policy a decade later: its aims were peace in the area followed by commercial expansion. Undoubtedly, Pile's plan was inspired by these objectives. It promised a better deal for the foreign claimants, although at the same time it clearly placed the republic under U.S. tutelage. Hard to swallow for an independent country, it was more so for a ruler such as Guzmán Blanco, the unusually arrogant leader of a country with an awakening national consciousness. However, the U.S. suggestions had the merit of catapulting the Venezuelan government into considering other proposals. Guzmán Blanco realized that in order to stay out of international trouble he had to permit some semblance of a debate. Joint deliberations with the foreign envoys involved finally resulted in an agreement which became law, November 30, 1872. Basically, this meant that it could not be terminated by unilateral decision.[27] It affirmed some voice for foreign powers in Venezuelan financial administration with regard to the "diplomatic debts", but it is doubtful if the diplomats realized that this voice could only be heard jointly; if not it would be lost in the desert.[28] But for the time being tensions caused by the "diplomatic debts" were eased.

The Dutch/Antillian claims were included in the general agreement but their size had yet to be decided. Unfortunately for the claimants, Caracas would make this decision. In one of the first meetings between Brakel and Guzmán, the latter coolly pointed out that some of the Dutch claims were grossly inflated through bribery or deceit, and he expressed his confidence that the Dutch government would agree to a revision.[29]

The demands of the Jesurun House formed the lion's share of the Dutch/Antillian claims. They were divided between old ones dating before April 27, 1870 (the day Guzmán Blanco took over), incurred in loans and trade with alternating Yellow and Blue governments, and new ones resulting from the seizure of the *Honfleur* and the *Sarah* and the arrest of Abraham J. Jesurun. There was some serious doubt from the Venezuelans about some of the enormous bill's items. By adding a monthly interest of $1\frac{1}{4}$ per cent, old claims had increased to 585,509,55 *venezolanos* or 1,171,019,10 Dutch guilders by March 31, 1873. With the assurance of diplomatic intervention the firm had padded this claim with some new items: 60,000 *venezolanos* for damages caused by the seizure of the *Honfleur*, 10,000 *venezolanos* for damages caused by the seizure of the *Sarah*, and 250,000 *venezolanos* for damages caused by the arrest of Jesurun and losses to his firm. Thus the total claim of the Jesurun House incurred after April 27, 1870 came to 320,000 *venezolanos*.[30] Some time later the damages caused by Jesurun's arrest, first estimated at 100,000 *venezolanos* (included in the above-mentioned 250,000 *venezolanos*) increased to 140,000, bringing the total new claim to 360,000 *venezolanos* or 720,000 guilders.[31] The old and new claims of the Jesurun House combined amounted to 845,509,55 *venezolanos* or 1,891,019,10 guilders, not including the 1¼ per cent interest the Curaçao firm thought it could rightfully add to its new claims.

The talks between the extensively-instructed Brakel and the Venezuelan government were hampered by an accumulation of complaints about the revolutionary activities of Venezuelan exiles in Curaçao — now, of course, belonging to the anti-*guzmancista* or Blue group — and complicated by seizures of Dutch ships. These irritations will be discussed in the next chapter. They did not seriously interrupt the negotiations since both sides were eager to maintain a dialogue, but other problems arose.

In early 1873, the Venezuelan Congress adopted some laws concerning foreigners. They stipulated that "foreigners who take part in Venezuela's civil strifes lose the right to claim compensation for damages incurred by military or other actions." [32] The real implications of these laws in connection with foreign claims did not escape the attention of the parties involved, and several countries protested. U.S. minister Pile seemed to have received instructions "to protest unofficially against some articles", and he stated that "their application will not be silently accepted by the U.S." [33] Great Britain objected in more general terms.

Confronted with these protests the Guzmán Blanco regime, well aware of the lack of cooperation among the interested powers, did not yield. The French, who considered the new laws "not unjust", assured it their support. But France had a separate agreement with Venezuela, dating back to 1856, which was very advantageous to her claimants, and for this reason did not protest.[34] Italy foresaw difficulties but also refrained from protest, probably in order not to irritate the Great Liberal.[35]

The Jesurun House, accused of siding with the enemies of the Guzmán Blanco regime, was maneuvered into a peculiar position. It had lost any right to make claims according to the new laws. The *Opinión Nacional,* the fervent propaganda tool of the liberal regime, stated this sarcastically in an article justifying the official position: foreigners had no right to compensation in cases where this same right was denied to inhabitant natives.[36] This self-righteous declaration manifested a feeling erupting not only in Venezuela but in the whole of South America, denying foreigners any extra rights and putting them on a par with other inhabitants. Somewhat earlier, the Calvo Doctrine had provided a more concise formula for this feeling.

In this atmosphere and against the background of the government's aforementioned proposals, Brakel's negotiations on Dutch claims with Guzmán's successor, D. B. Barrios, were far from easy.[37] The Jesurun claims were suddenly placed on delicate grounds. Making it very clear that it considered some of the items inflated, the Venezuelan government rejected the greater part in plain terms. It was equally reluctant to accept the high interest rate. It did not reject earlier agreements with Dutch/Antillean claimants, however, such as one concluded through Rolandus November 10, 1869, in which a Jesurun claim of 347,706,26 *venezolanos* was recognized.[38] Brakel had to compromise in a drastic way: the Jesurun claim was almost cut in half before agreement was reached to include it in the "diplomatic debts".

Jesurun's lawyer in Holland, Van Eck, protested.[39] In this man, the Curaçao firm found a potent advocate of its cause. As a member of the Second Chamber he could ask any minister embarrassing questions, and he did.

In January, 1874, the Venezuelan government appointed a special plenipotenciary, Alejandro Goiticoa, to discuss with Brakel some remaining difficulties and to finalize "a friendly settlement of the pending claims".[40] With this official, Brakel was able to come to what Venezuela called satisfactory conclusions of his negotiations. The decimated claims of the Jesurun House, together with those of two other Jewish merchants, Jeudah Senior and Isaac Pardo, were finally accepted and included in the regular file of the "diplomatic debts".

Of course, the Venezuelan-Dutch negotiations did not stand apart from similar arrangements with other creditors of the republic. Neither political nor economic pressure seemed to have played a role in their conclusion, and no interests were seriously endangered. Payments, suspended since April, 1870, now would be resumed in August, 1873, after an interruption of nearly three and a half years. If in many cases claims were drastically reduced, the feeling among the claimants seemed to be that half a loaf was better than none. As Guzmán Blanco announced in his message to Congress of 1873, the following items concerning foreign claims were decided:

a. 13 per cent of each 40 units of national income would be used to pay the "diplomatic debts".
b. English claims would be paid up to the amount settled by a commission already appointed in 1868 (awaiting approval of Congress).
c. French claims would be paid as usual, but the amount was inflated and had to be redefined.
d. Danish claims were completely recognized and would be paid.
e. Spanish claims needed revision.
f. Italian claims would be excluded from participation in the 13 per cent.
g. Dutch claims, as far as they were discussed with the Dutch chargé d'affaires, amounted to 400,000 *pesos* or *venezolanos* [800,000 guilders]. Some of them were still under investigation.
h. Claims of the U.S. were under discussion by a commission appointed in 1866. It was discovered, however, that error and bribery had inflated the amount. The Venezuelan Congress was called to make a decision, the U.S. being disinclined to accept a revision of the aforementioned commission's decision.[41]

No reliable proof casts doubt on Guzmán Blanco's sincere intent to solve the debt problems; some delicately applied pressure was helpful, however, in reminding him of his government's obligation to start payments, as when representatives of Great Britain, Italy, the Netherlands, the United States, and Germany sent a joint note expressing their impatience.[42] This note, indeed, was a mild variant of a much stronger show of force suggested two years earlier to the Dutch government by the Germans when difficulties with *guzmancista* Venezuela started.[43] It is probable that this note was the final inducement to the Venezuelan government to honor its obligations.

Thus payments were resumed August, 1875. The Venezuelan authorities followed the procedure indicated: 13 per cent of 40 per cent of the total revenue. For the first six months of 1873 this amounted to roughly 100,000 *venezolanos*. Of this sum was paid:

to Great Britain	14,500	*venezolanos*
to France	37,200	,,
to U.S.	18,400	,,
to the Netherlands	9,500	,,
to Spain	18,400	,,
to Denmark	2,000	,,

The quota were paid in monthly installments to the foreign envoys who distributed them among the claimants. For the time being financial disputes had been settled.

8. THE TRANQUIL YEAR 1873

Brakel's arrival in Caracas promised to initiate a period of tranquil relations between Venezuela and the Netherlands (with her Curaçao colony). The satisfactory progress of his negotiations regarding claims of the Jewish creditors was — in spite of the severe cuts in those claims — a favorable omen.

This tranquility existed only on the surface. Ceaseless complaints by the Venezuelan government of violations of the Royal Decree of 1871 continued to accumulate on Wagner's desk. The island, they repeated, was a focal point of conspiracy and agitation against the Caracas government, while colonial authorities remained hostile or indifferent to Venezuelan interests. Two factors contributed to this feeling: a growing awareness of national independence, together with a realization that the political and economic situation of the republic was not as stable as its authoritarian leader wanted or pretended it to be. He had grown very sensitive to the role of Jewish smugglers and traders in war materiel and to the attitude of colonial authorities. Thus one may speculate that at the end of 1872 the Venezuelan Foreign Minister had this attitude of his country's president in mind when he assured the Dutch chargé d'affaires that "Venezuela enjoyed a complete tranquility," but added somewhat ruefully that "the dissatisfied try their hardest to involve the republic again in a civil strife. The island of Curaçao is close. There they publish their seditious pamphlets ... doing everything they would do in hostile territory." [1]

This observation leads us again to the core of the problem as Guzmán Blanco visualized it at that time. The apparently good relations between his government and the Dutch induced Barrios to make a frank statement (of some stifling details) outlining the possible disastrous effect on the republic resulting from failure to enforce the Royal Decree of 1871. More efficient control was badly needed to stop punishable actions like those undertaken by the Dutch schooner *La Gracia de Dios,* purchased or chartered from Jewish merchant, Jeudah Senior, by Venezuelan Blue general, J. M. Pirela Sutil. Although this plan to bring war materiel to Puerto Cabello was prematurely discovered, the dangerous cargo still had escaped the arm of the Dutch port officials. It had been transferred in open sea to another Dutch schooner, the *Manuelita* (owner David Haim Salas, Curaçao), also purchased or chartered by Pirela Sutil. This ship was seized in Puerto Cabello and brought to Coro. Most disturbing to Venezuelan exiles in Curaçao and their relatives and friends in the republic was the seizure of many brochures and letters revealing the names of some conspirators, among them the civilians Felipe Larrazábal, Rafael Hermoso, and Luis Mantel Baralt together with those of the generals Ignacio Galán, José María Pirela Sutil, and Antonio Mendoza.[2]

Clearly affected by this discovery, the Venezuelan Foreign Minister pointed out to Brakel that his country's interests were gravely endangered by these alleged conspiracies. Brakel, under strict orders, asked for proof. "Those proofs are in Curaçao," retorted an angry Barrios. "My information is oral." He nevertheless promised the Dutch chargé d'affaires to support his accusations. But at the same time forgetting, purposefully or not, the niceties of nineteenth century diplomatic courtesy, he added an open threat:

"If the colonial government was not willing to end the conspiring activities of the exiles and the exportation of war materiel once and for all, the Venezuelan government would resort to more effective means to defend itself, i.e., to close the coastal ports to all commercial relations with Curaçao,"

because, as he explained, "if not, Venezuela would certainly suffer another civil war."[3]

Brakel was well aware of the ominous attitude of the Venezuelan minister. The latter had made his point very convincingly: without commercial relations Curaçao's prosperity was doomed. This awareness seems to have pushed the Dutch chargé d'affaires to accept without second thought the Venezuelan presentation of the facts. He deemed it absolutely necessary that the prerogatives of the Governor of Curaçao be broadened to enable him to expel from colonial territory without specific orders from The Hague any foreigner who threatened relations with the republic.

It is questionable whether Brakel realized the range of such an instruction. As acting Attorney General of the island, Salomon Senior had already observed as early as 1870: "If one wants to expel those exiles who participate in the disorders of their country, that measure would extend to almost all exiles because without a doubt the vast majority is involved in them." Distinctly impressed by his long discussions with Barrios, Brakel wrote with some dark premonition that

> "it is now certain that Curaçao, as a result of revolutionary agitation and intrigues of the Venezuelan refugees, will be threatened with measures of reprisal. What advantage brings their presence to the island? Capital? Labor? Morality? None of these." [4]

During the last months of the year, Barrios came up with more complaints. Pedro José Rojas, for instance, a prominent civilian of the Blue faction, imprisoned for several months by Guzmán Blanco despite of his bad health, was finally set free. He fled to Curaçao, where he was welcomed enthusiastically by his fellow refugees. Mistaking colonial hospitality for a license to scheme, he issued a ridiculous proclamation against the Great Liberal, followed by an order of the day in which he exhorted all Venezuelans to join him as their leader.[5] "The exiles," Barrios exclaimed, "hold many meetings in Hotel Americano and I am ordered by my president to insist that strong measures be taken." [6]

Brakel's reports, conspicuously sympathetic to the Venezuelan arguments, resulted in an order to Wagner to forbid all political activities and demonstrations by foreigners. To facilitate executing such a strong measure The Hague decided to send an extra man-of-war to Curaçao.[7] Brakel was instructed to explain the Dutch response to Venezuelan demands.[8] Simultaneously, however, the Dutch Foreign Minister admonished the chargé d'affaires to moderate his zeal for the Venezuelan point of view and to try to understand the problems of the colonial authorities.

Thus the Governor of Curaçao, furnished with broader instructions and bowing to Caracas' demands, expelled Pirela Sutil.[9] The Venezuelan protested but to no avail. He left the island January 7, 1873, destined for Santo Domingo. Venezuela responded very favorably to this expulsion but her suspicions of a conspiracy were visibly strengthened.

If the Dutch had expected some increase of goodwill, they certainly were soon deeply disappointed. The compromising letters referred to earlier, mentioned the names of many prominent exiles. Barrios' favorable reaction soon evaporated, and new demands requested the expulsion of three other refugees: Felipe Larrazábal, and generals Facundo Camero and Ignacio Galán. The Governor of Curaçao, much against his personal conviction, again bowed to pressure and complied with the request.

Wagner was the more unhappy because he suspected that the Dutch chargé d'affaires in Caracas was somehow behind the matter. Later a fifth refugee followed. This was José Aniceto Serrano, in the words of Wagner "a meddlesome, difficult man, in league with the followers of Mr. Sassen." [10] For Serrano the order of expulsion was tragic. He was married to a Dutch woman and had lived in Curaçao for over 25 years. Much against his will he was forced to leave.[11] General Galán was allowed to remain on the island until March 7 because of illness.[12]

Again a calmer period was expected. After the required consultation with Brakel and the Colonial *Raad,* at the end of January, 1873, the Governor of Curaçao suspended the Royal Decree of 1871. The Venezuelan government, placated by several expulsions, did not object.[13] Guzmán Blanco responded publicly to this measure in his message to the Venezuelan Congress of February 20, 1873: "First Holland and then Spain have realized the fairness with which we have maintained our friendly relations through representatives who interpret these relations in an honest way." [14]

Wagner's bitter feelings also mellowed somewhat, especially because of the ministerial warning directed at Brakel, whose pro-Venezuelan attitude was beginning to annoy the governor. It was the latter's conviction that the refugees were expelled not so much as a result of their conspiracies as of Guzmán Blanco's personal vendetta. In leaving the island they had indignantly declared that if they ever came to power Brakel would immediately be declared *persona non grata.*[15]

Almost overnight Brakel had become a very popular figure in Caracas, warmly received by the Guzmán Blanco officials. That "he has made himself a very good position in the good society of Caracas," was even known to Lucio Pulido in Paris.[16] The "good society" was, of course, the *guzmancista* faction.

The Venezuelan government's willingness to initiate negotiations on a mercantile treaty with the Netherlands, to improve the inadequate regulation of 1830, illustrated this high standing of the Dutch chargé d'affaires. The Hague was requested to commission him to represent the Dutch side.[17]

The honeymoon was a short one.

9. THE CURAÇAO COMMITTEE

A few tiny clouds appeared in the blue sky over Venezuela and Curaçao at the beginning of 1874, heralds of bigger ones to come. A new rebellion was to threaten Guzmán Blanco's peace preached with the sword and set off a chain reaction of tense events. The discovery that arms and ammunition used against the Great Liberal's armed forces in a minor revolt had been smuggled from Curaçao via Río de la Hacha in Colombia to the State of Zulia became the first sore point of friction.[1] It then became known in Caracas that the Jesurun House had concluded a loan for the purchase of war materiel with the anti-*guzmancista* general in exile, Luis Level de Goda. Finally, a certain General Luis M. Díaz, a Venezuelan refugee in Curaçao who directed an educational institution called Colegio Vargas, had placed an advertisement in the *Curaçaosche Courant* considered offensive by the Venezuelan government.[2]

A strong note, obviously dictated by Guzmán Blanco himself although signed by the new Foreign Minister, Jesús M. Blanco, marked the first of new complaints and destroyed the relaxed mood prevailing at the end of the previous year.

> "The closeness of the island of Curaçao," the note said, "to the coast of Venezuela is the cause that said island is destined by the enemies of the peace of the republic to buy their war materiel necessary for the realization of their plans there ... Curaçao will constitute a constant threat for the peace of the republic if the colonial authorities do not take effective measures to stop what repeats itself daily." [3]

Regarding the rumor of the Jesurun loan — which probably was true — the Venezuelan government retaliated with a suspension of payments. Cries of injustice from A. J. Jesurun himself[4] and an immediate action in The Hague by the firm's lawyer, Van Eck, alerted the Dutch government to the renewed tensions.[5]

As for Díaz, the Venezuelan government resorted to a familiar tactic and requested his expulsion. In discussing this problem with Blanco who displayed little inclination to leniency, Brakel received additional proof of Díaz' supposed "criminal intentions". The Venezuelan minister angrily showed Brakel a letter allegedly written by Díaz, although the signature was A. Tejada. Other letters, however, were produced, written and signed by Díaz. Brakel handed them to a Dutch graphologist who assured him that they were all in the same hand.[6]

The Governor of Curaçao, doubtless burdened by these irrefutable facts, was seriously concerned that the situation might get out of hand and ordered an immediate investigation into the smugglers' circumvention of island regulations. The outcome was revealing. The schooner *Lamia,* for instance, owned by Venezuelan inhabitants of the State of Zulia but sailing under Dutch flag had, on one of its filibustering expeditions, disembarked war materiel in Río de la Hacha (Colombia). Dutch port authorities had given official permission for the export because of the destination. Satisfactory assurance had been given — in accordance with the regulation of 1858, since the Royal Degree of 1871 was suspended — that export would not take place to rebellious regions. The schooner arrived at Río de la Hacha, unloaded its cargo, and as Wagner observed, what occurred later was no longer the concern of the Curaçao authorities. Colombian officials seized the cargo at the request of the local Venezuelan consul, before it was on its way to Venezuela.[7]

A similar incident had occurred with the *Paquete Arubano,* which had unloaded 300 rifles and other war materiel in the same port. Back in Curaçao when questioned by the Attorney General, the captain gave the improbable explanation that he had thrown all cargo overboard because of leakage and had been forced to disembark his passengers — all refugees — somewhere on the Venezuelan coast.[8]

These and other incidents demonstrate the techniques of circumventing the law to make huge profits at the cost of increasing friction between the island and the republic. They definitely widened the rift between Wagner and Brakel. Wagner had built for himself an excellent reputation as an efficient administrator and disciplined subordinate of The Hague. In clashing with a more independently-minded Brakel he adopted a realistic and conservative attitude in accordance with the views of the Minister for the Colonies. "Venezuela requests that no export of war materiel should take place other than with the knowledge of her government," he wrote his chief. "It is impossible to satisfy that demand." Why it would be impossible is simple: it would be contrary to the sacred principle of free trade, the venerated essence of European liberal economic theory. Wagner could perceive only one exception to this principle: if Venezuela should become involved in a war or if two belligerent parties existed in the country during civil strife.[9] He rejected the existence of two such parties at that moment.

A look at the experience of other islands will place the Curaçao case in a larger context. The Danish government of St. Thomas, for instance, did not permit the export of any war materiel without the permission of the consul of that nation to which it was destined. This attitude was laid down in consular agreements with several nations including Venezuela.

However, the incredible fact remained that the Netherlands had not included the Curaçao colony in the consular agreement with Venezuela concluded in 1830.[10] Hence, there was no recognized Venezuelan consul in Willemstad. The so-called commercial agents were only accepted as tokens of good-will and to smooth relations, not as official appointees of their government. "But even if this were so," wrote the Curaçao governor, "I would not be a defender of the obligation that a foreign consul must give his consent." Wagner saw this as an empty gesture. "He who exports war materiel, knowing that he would never get a permit from the consul in question, would certainly provide himself with a permit from another consul, falsify his papers, or buy a permit." A possible solution was suggested: the obligation to show official papers which would prove that war materiel really was disembarked in the pretended port of destination.

The governor's answer touched upon the root of European liberal views. Dutch metropolitan politicians and their agents in Curaçao were firm believers in this principle of free trade, thinking almost exclusively of the importance of overseas markets for their commercial ventures, especially for the islands, and overlooking or minimizing political implications. These politicians, Wagner included, became export-oriented to such a degree that they subordinated all other problems to the maintenance of this honored principle, even at the risk of diplomatic rupture. Wagner's unsophisticated economic analysis reflects this myopic view perfectly. The principle of free trade was a sacred cow to be saved at the expense of all other principles.

Brakel did not profess the same feeling. "This principle of free trade," he argued, "voluntarily adopted by the colony, was certainly not chosen to cause its decline." Rightly or wrongly, as he wrote the Dutch Foreign Minister, Venezuela saw the traffic in war materiel from Curaçao as a great danger to be averted at all costs. In effect she said to Curaçao: if you give up this traffic, my ports will be open to you. If you don't, I will take measures to protect myself.

These measures, Brakel continued, would cause the destruction of Curaçao's vulnerable economy: an obnoxious and hateful obstruction to Dutch vessels entering Venezuelan ports, the closing of some of these ports, and perhaps the introduction of a differential right of 25 per cent on all commodities originating from the Curaçao islands.[11]

Brakel's argument was strong. "I am a champion of free trade," he wrote. But in view of the island's economic dependence upon trade with Venezuela, he asked, what was the wisest thing to do? For him it was a rhetorical question.

In spite of these problems Guzmán Blanco, in his message to Congress, March 13, 1874, did not draw a discouraging picture with regard to the Netherlands. He knowingly ignored the exciting issues and limited himself to generalities: "Venezuela lives in peace and harmony with all other countries," he said and solemnly predicted that "although there are some problems to be resolved, these take a tranquil course and will be solved in a fair agreement." [12]

Repeated discussions with Blanco in which the Venezuelan Foreign Minister insisted on Díaz's expulsion convinced the Dutch chargé d'affaires that it would perhaps not be just but certainly in the best interests of the island to sacrifice this refugee. Blanco's repeated threats against Curaçao's economy did not fail to influence Brakel. Added to that impression were fears: Blanco casually mentioned a Venezuelan offer to international steamship companies to include one or more Venezuelan ports in their itineraries on the condition that no ship of such company would anchor in Curaçao.[13] Whatever Brakel though of Díaz's guilt was no longer important. His fear of Venezuelan retaliation was.[14]

In sharp contrast to this state of mind was the attitude of the Governor of Curaçao. "The position of the Venezuelan government," he wrote, "offends the dignity of the Dutch government. It makes the expulsion of Díaz almost impossible." [15] "To hell with dignity," retorted Brakel, "you have to eat, don't you?" But Wagner was not inclined to give in to what he defined as blackmail, convinced as he was that with the expulsion of Díaz, Guzmán Blanco's demands would only increase.[16] Probably not aware of the striking changes in the republic, he did not realize that the Venezuelan dictator had the firm support of the Caracas merchants, who were only too happy to help him eliminate a prosperous middleman and ruin a dangerous competitor.[17]

The new wave of demands created some concern in the Netherlands where difficulties in the East Indies had previously absorbed almost all attention. Discussions on the Venezuelan Question proceeded erratically for several months. Finally, the Dutch Cabinet arrived at a decision in which Wagner's views prevailed at the expense of Brakel's. The latter was curtly informed that the Dutch government "could not carry out the desire of the Venezuelan government." [18] Díaz could stay.

One of the Venezuelan government's assessments had been correct: the *Lamia* and the *Paquete Arubano* incidents pointed toward a rebellion conceived on Curaçao. On October 17 of that year it exploded in Coro, masterminded by General León Colina, and it took Guzmán Blanco three long, bloody months to suppress it.[19] *Guzmancista* units of the weak Venezuelan fleet blockaded the rebellious port and the coast of the State of Falcón. The Dutch government, for once accurately estimating the effects of this policy on its colonial possessions sent two men-of-war to Willemstad to reinforce the ship already stationed there.

At the end of October, Wagner received his first information on the revolt, two weeks after it had started. Why Brakel, who knew about it from the start, failed to inform the Governor of Curaçao remains a mystery. The omission would have disastrous consequences. As soon as he was informed, Wagner repealed his decision of January 29, 1873. The Royal Decree of 1871 was once again in effect. A stiff warning was issued to all merchants, shipowners, captains, and crews not to become involved in the republic's crisis at the risk of transgressing island regulations and exposing themselves to prosecution.[20]

The decision, too late to appease the Guzmán Blanco regime, was an empty gesture in the dilemma of controlling the export trade. The rebels had already been provided with what they needed and they had received ample credit for their undertakings. Venezuela's Foreign Minister roared that "Curaçao had carried out an action which cannot fail to make a very disagreeable impression upon His Excellency the President of the Republic." [21] Already earlier, Blanco had openly accused the island of being "a constant threat" to the peace of Venezuela. Curaçao in his words was the center, "the foyer of a conspiracy" against the constitutional government of Venezuela. It was the headquarters of a revolution which it had financed.[22] This revolution was the brainchild, Blanco continued, of Díaz and financed by what he called "the Curaçao Committee".[23] The most prominent members of this committee were, besides Díaz, some Curaçao merchants: the two partners of the Jesurun House, Oduber,[24] Hendrick Evertsz, J. R.

Mendes, former commercial agent of the republic who had deserted to the anti-*guzmancistas,* a son and partner of Jeudah Senior (who himself stayed neutral) and some refugees from Venezuela — the generals Colina, Fernando Adames, José Gregorio Riera, Ramón Rivas, Romualdo Falcón, and a few others.

Blanco's formal statement accused the Curaçao members of this committee of having financed the revolt by giving credit to its Venezuelan members and selling them the hardware at good prices. All requests to move "that rock", i.e., Curaçao, into taking effective measures against the exiles had met, Blanco indignantly pointed out, with rebuffs.[25] They had made the island an arsenal for the enemies of the republic. Emphasizing this argument again and again he accused The Hague of protecting Jesurun and other Curaçao merchants, who out of speculative greed and a criminal lust for profit supplied the "treacherous conspirators" with arms to shed the blood of Venezuelan citizens. Díaz was not expelled, although his participation in the preparation of the revolt was proven. Was this not proof of The Hague's complicity? Wagner was, unquestionably, a silent accomplice of Curaçao's unscrupulous traders. Blanco's indignant blasts finally came to the point. An indemnity would be demanded for all losses suffered in this rebellion. On orders of the angry president, the data for this procedure were being gathered. In the meantime, the Venezuelan government protested vehemently against the participation of Curaçao in her internal strife and against authorities — here Wagner was meant — who collaborated openly or silently with the unscrupulous.[26]

Cautious not to throw more oil on the flames, Brakel postponed an indignant denial on the pretext that he had to wait for instructions. Candor is the wrong catalyst for diplomatic discussions, as he was unhappily aware. The arrival of a Dutch squadron in the Caribbean — mentioned in the previous chapter — would also be too alarming to be swallowed with equanimity and so was kept secret.

What else could the Dutch chargé d'affaires do? To appease the rising clamor of the Venezuelans he sent Blanco a copy of the *Curaçaosche Courant* with Wagner's decision to reintroduce the Royal Decree of 1871.[27] Much too late, sneered the Foreign Minister.

The situation deteriorated further with the *Midas* question. On October 30, 1874, the Venezuelan port authorities of Cumaná seized the Dutch schooner *Midas* (owner Jesurun House).[28] It may have been the flagship of the small squadron of three or four ships fitted out by the Curaçao Committee. This was maintained by the Venezuelans.

The erratic behavior of the *Midas* sparked new waves of deepening indignation.

The schooner had left Curaçao on October 24, a week after the rebellion in Coro had exploded but before Wagner was officially informed. It had left Willemstad with a cargo of rifles and eight chests of ammunition. This was approved because the ship's destination was given as Trinidad, and the Royal Degree of 1871 was not yet in force. Besides the regular crew of 10 or 12 men, it carried aboard a passenger, the mysterious Waldemar Worm, mysterious because nothing is known about him except that he paid 1,000 guilders for a trip which could easily have been made by regular steamship connections for one tenth the price and much more comfortably.[29] A humorous and significant detail was the fact that the schooner, while leaving Curaçao's St. Ann Bay and saluting the Amsterdam fortress, passed Abraham J. Jesurun and the turncoat Mendes standing in front of it.

The *Midas* sailed from Willemstad to Bonaire and from there to Barcelona on the Venezuelan coast, presumably waiting for another vessel to which it could transfer its war materiel. The other ship never showed up.[30] The schooner then sailed to Tortuga (also on the Venezuelan coast) where it unloaded some of its cargo. The next morning it sailed to Punto de Araya. Here Mr. Worm disembarked with some papers but later reappeared. The *Midas* then sailed to the island of Coche where it anchored. Mr. Worm disembarked again, now with four chests of ammunition and two of rifles. He returned after some time and the voyage was resumed to Cumaná, where they arrived late in the afternoon of October 30.

The *Midas* entered the port of Cumaná, its captain declared, for fresh water. Although he knew that Guzmán Blanco had closed that port for international trade, he claimed that it was an emergency. The port authorities seized the ship, allegedly for violating orders of the president and for carrying war materiel. The crew members were tied together like criminals, the captain, the boatswain, and Mr. Worm being the only ones allowed to ride mules while they passed through the streets of Caracas to be imprisoned.[31] Very little food was served, and thus the few coins that had escaped the sharp eyes of the greedy guards were used to buy provisions. Some members of the crew later showed scars and claimed to have been mistreated.[32]

Brakel protested. At the time the *Midas* left Curaçao, he pointed out, the Coro rebellion was not yet known there. "Here is no crime nor delict," he wrote Blanco, "therefore the traffic in war materiel was still free and legal." [33] Realizing, however, that his position threatened to become somewhat ambiguous with Wagner's and the Jesurun House's accusations of his pro-Venezuelan outlook, he accepted the risk of adding to the souring relations and informed Blanco of the Dutch squadron's mission.[34] The Venezuelan reacted bitterly and sarcastically with outcries of high emotional voltage.

Wagner asserted himself with more coolness and decision and less fear than Brakel. Upon hearing of the seizure of the *Midas*, he sent the *Julieta*, sailing under British flag but possibly another unit of the Curaçao Committee's squadron, to Cumaná to investigate. The Jesuruns were clearly disappointed. They preferred sending the Dutch man-of-war from Curaçao, to intimidate the Venezuelans with some "muscle showing".[35]

It required no prophet to predict what would happen. The *Julieta* was also seized, not only because she entered a closed Venezuelan port but also because it irritated Guzmán Blanco that the Curaçao governor tried to obtain information about the *Midas* from subordinate local officials instead of going through diplomatic channels.[36]

The recurrent tensions were amplified by the hostile Venezuelan press, with the *Opinión Nacional* playing a leading role. This mouthpiece of the regime showed strong anti-Curaçao feelings in a trenchant article written in December: "Curaçao can only survive because of our disgrace. It feeds itself as a crow on our spoils, it is a tumor which thrives on us and grows only for the morbid condition of the being to which it is attached." These vilifying expressions set the tone for more: "Curaçao is the tape worm of our social body, it devours the substance of the Republic and keeps her in perpetual convulsion," with the obvious conclusion: "Let Curaçao disappear." [37]

Somewhat later the *Gaceta Oficial* published a resolution which ordered public treasury officials to open a separate account of the expenses caused by the present rebellion, thus showing that Guzmán Blanco meant business with his threat to bill the Dutch for the revolt. The *Opinión Nacional* reprinted it under the provocative heading: "Todo será Justicia".

Rumors intensified fears of the threatening conflict. Guzmán Blanco, it was whispered, not only planned the presentation of a fat bill to the Dutch, but also a surprise attack on Curaçao with a fleet of six ships and 5,000 men. Wagner communicated this incredible possibility to The Hague. The Dutch Foreign Minister remained cool, like his governor, belittling the threats to Curaçao's vulnerable position in terms of Venezuelan military action and correctly asserting that the aggressive president was far too occupied with subduing the rebellion in his own country, to have time for such an attack. Wagner was not so sure. Guzmán Blanco, he wrote, was known for his unpredictability. In case of a defeat in his own country, he might turn in desperation to a raid against the island. He had never forgotten the humiliation of 1870. But the Dutch governor felt confident that he could easily stop any Venezuelan invasion with the one ironclad he had at his disposal.[38]

10. THE DUTCH SQUADRON

In the mounting tensions between Curaçao and Venezuela, the Dutch legal position was not a strong one. The rebellion in Coro was undoubtedly masterminded in and supported from Curaçao. That the Venezuelan government blamed the lackadaisical attitude of colonial authorities and the hard-headed policy of The Hague for this revolt was understandable. The existence of a revolutionary committee residing in the colony and operating with the persistent backing of the Caribbean "Rothschilds" and other wealthy Jewish merchants was documented by too many witnesses to be denied. It therefore seemed incredible that the Dutch Foreign Minister dismissed these accusations as fantasies and took the serious threats of the Guzmán Blanco regime lightheartedly. The seizure of the *Midas* only slightly concerned him. Three possibilities for this seizure were dismissed: violation of the Venezuelan blockade announced after the eruption of the Coro rebellion; illicit transportation of war materiel; or the participation in a rebellion against the Venezuelan government. The chargé d'affaires in Caracas was ordered to request immediate restitution of the ship and compensation for losses suffered by its illegal seizure.[1] The commander of the Dutch squadron plowing the Atlantic toward the West Indies was instructed to seize the *Midas* and bring the schooner to Curaçao in case the Venezuelan government refused to return it. If he could not find the ship, he was allowed to capture one or two Venezuelan vessels and bring those to Willemstad as bargaining tools.[2]

It seems that The Hague sincerely believed that direct threat of military force could be effective. It never realized that the presence of Dutch naval power with offensive intentions in Venezuelan waters would infuriate as well as humiliate the Venezuelans.

But The Hague had drawn the directives. If, in the emerging crisis, force were needed, Brakel should be prepared to ask for his passport and leave the country quickly to avoid the situation in which Rolandus found himself in 1870. A more vigorous Dutch attitude preferred to break relations for humiliating expulsion. In weighing these alternatives the Dutch Cabinet acknowledged that a war situation would be most unwelcome. Although sympathising with the island's merchants and their predicament, the Minister for the Colonies tried at the same time to discover the truth about certain rumors and ordered Governor Wagner to investigate the financial manipulations of the Jesurun House and other businessmen. Wagner had already sent the one man-of-war at his disposal to Coro in order to investigate Guzmán Blanco's definition of a blockade. The Dutch man-of-war made two trips — December 21 and 29 — but did not encounter any blockading vessels. A reassured governor then concluded that Guzmán Blanco's bite was not as bad as his bark and that his blockade was a paper one.[3]

A new diversion occurred in late November when the Coro rebels seized the Venezuelan schooner *Bolivita* and promptly used it to communicate with their island headquarters. That this was possible without interference by colonial authorities caused a fresh upsurge of *guzman-cista* anger. The latter also permitted another schooner, the *Enero de 74,* to leave port carrying aboard the revolutionary generals Ignacio Galán (expelled before but back with or without the permission of Wagner), Teófilo Celis, Emiliano Hernández, and others. Rumors added that the schooner carried 6,000 pounds of gunpowder destined for Santo Domingo. Instead, the ship sailed for Coro.[4]

The vehemence of new civil strife and the widespread strength of subversive movements in the republic increased the irritability of its Caracas leaders. Thus more grievances were brought to Brakel's attention. One of the most convincing concerned the *Elvinia.*[5] This Dutch schooner had sailed from St. Thomas, cleared there by the consul of Santo Domingo, destined for this republic. Two days later the Curaçao Committee contacted the *Elvinia*'s captain and ordered him to sail to Coro. Because of the refusal of the crew to be exposed to the dangers of Venezuela's civil war, the Committee fitted out the *Colibri* (owner Jesurun House) which took over the *Elvinia*'s cargo in open sea. The *Colibri* then disposed of the war materiel in Coro and returned to Curaçao. It seems that all of the Curaçao Committee's operations were accomplished in this complicated way.[6]

The arrogance and abuses of some Curaçao merchants provided enough material for more grievances. There was the case of the *Isabel* (owner Jesurun House), sailing from Curaçao with war materiel destined for Santo Domingo. Somehow the ship arrived in Coro.[7] A similar thing happened to the *Indiana* (owner unknown), which left Santo Domingo with 57 chests containing 1,120 rifles, destination Curaçao, which also dropped anchor in Coro. When news arrived of striking rebel victories, the Curaçao Committee planned to send three or four ships with 5,000 rifles, much ammunition and gunpowder, and many uniforms to Coro.[8] How all this could be managed under Wagner's nose without his being aware of it is inexplicable.

All these facts pointed to an obvious conclusion which the Venezuelan government was not slow to reach: colonial authorities patronized the trade in war materiel and protected the activities of the Curaçao Committee, thus identifying themselves with the Coro rebels and contributing to civil disorder in the republic.[9] Since Curaçao seemed unwilling to impose tougher control on export of war materiel and Caracas did not have a strong war fleet, Guzmán Blanco was compelled to find other means to counteract the apparent inability of the colonial authorities to stop this trade and to eliminate the hostile activities of the Curaçao Committee.

At the beginning of November payments on loans to the Jesurun House were suspended. Brakel, who received these payments was requested to return the sums already received and still under his control. As long as Jesurun acted as a belligerent, Guzmán Blanco said, he was not willing to pay his enemies.[10] Softening, however, this rather abrupt stand in order to improve his own image, the self-worshipping president decided that "out of respect for the Dutch nation" these sums would not be returned to the Venezuelan treasury but would be used to pay off the claims of two other Curaçao creditors, Senior and Pardo, who were not involved in hostile activities.[11] Brakel rejected the suggestion.

Although Guzmán Blanco grumbled his satisfaction at Wagner's reinstatement of the Royal Decree of 1871, the latter's refusal to permit the export of war materiel belonging to the Venezuelan government soured the already bitter mood of the Illustrious American.[12] The special ship sent to pick up this materiel returned empty, a new injury to his highly sensitive ego. The realization that two Dutch men-of-war were approaching the Caribbean area and that they, together with the man-of-war at Willemstad and the one from Paramaribo (Surinam), could keep his coast under effective control undoubtedly added to his already bad spirits. His press vented these feelings. In one of the many contemptuous articles of the *Opinión Nacional,* the official irritation aimed mainly at Jesurun showed the hardening of this feeling: "possessed by the fury of insolence he throws everything in our fire, and spends money to encourage rebellion." [13] The publication of *El Imparcial* in Curaçao, edited by the "deserter" José Ramón Henríquez, a former *guzmancista,* was an additional source of official annoyance. From the

Civilisadó, an irregular weekly paper also published in Curaçao, Wagner learned that Venezuelan authorities had added the *Midas* to their small coast guard and ironically renamed the ship *Jesurum*.[14] Under this name the schooner was sent to Coro as part of a blockading squadron. In January, 1875, it seized the Dutch schooner *Colibri* which tried to break the blockade.[15] In spite of Wagner's evaluation it was not altogether a paper one.

The interlocking nature of the developments came to an end in February when the Coro rebellion was crushed, although some pockets of resistance continued to exist for many months. Guzmán Blanco's sensitivity on the Curaçao Committee question relaxed. Now he was able to pay more attention to his problems with the Netherlands and Great Britain, the latter country experiencing similar predicaments since Venezuela's capture of two British ships. There were also problems with Trinidad whose merchants played a role very much like Curaçao's.

In that same month the Dutch squadron finally arrived at Willemstad. Its commander immediately informed Brakel of his instruction, i.e., "to terminate the *Midas* question as quickly as possible." [16] It is highly doubtful if this sailor had the slightest understanding of the problem.

> "If we follow your advice," wrote Brakel to the captain, "to request the immediate release of the *Midas,* its crew, its passenger, plus 50,000 guilders, the arrogant president, now even more arrogant after his victory, will certainly refuse. What do you do then? You repeat the same request but you add a threat. The result will be that he gives me my passport and cuts off all relations." [17]

At the same time, Brakel wrote to Wagner informing him of Guzmán Blanco's attitude towards Great Britain and the experience of General Level de Goda who had supported the Coro revolution with a band of armed men from Trinidad.[18] The Dutch chargé d'affaires warned him emphatically to take Venezuelan threats against colonial trade seriously. The Venezuelan government was ready, he pointed out, to take unprecedented measures like closing the ports of Coro and Maracaibo, not only to punish these regions for their participation in the recent revolt — a measure highly popular with the Caracas merchants — but also to retaliate against Curaçao. "There is no doubt in my mind," he argued, "that this attitude would mean the end of the island's transit trade and thus an important source of income would dry up." [19]

Governor Wagner, a soldier by profession, was not as easily disturbed as Brakel and took an opposite point of view. "If the *Midas* has indeed been converted into a Venezuelan coast guard, the honor of the Dutch flag is involved," he answered. This argument was understood by the commander of the squadron. Both men favored ending the *Midas* question by force: seizing the *Midas* or one or two Venezuelan ships.

By now The Hague had become a little uneasy about the whole affair and offered subtle arguments to the world to prove Dutch good intentions. This attitude was clearly demonstrated in the Dutch Foreign Minister's circular letter to envoys in several capitals ordering them to inform the respective governments of Dutch problems in the Caribbean.[20] The understanding attitude of Great Britain seemed especially important. Lord Derby used this bait of sympathy — while scheming a South African conquest — to inform the Dutch minister in London of his impressions: the Venezuelan government probably was the worst and most provoking in the world. "Her Majesty's government," he added, "had as much reason as the Dutch to complain." He expressed no doubt that The Hague's grievances were well founded.[21]

This British reaction reinforced Brakel's flagging self-confidence. Lord Derby abstained from the use of force and the Dutch chargé d'affaires, sharply denying that the honor of the Dutch flag was involved, similarly focused all his attention on appeasement and reconciliation, while pointing out the disastrous consequences the use of force could bring.[22] To his new chief in The Hague — a Cabinet crisis there had resulted in a change of ministers — he wrote: "A fast solution of the *Midas* question is very desirable but the use of force will not achieve anything." When the investigation into the financial manipulations of the Jesurun House did not show anything wrong — it was conducted by the colonial Attorney General, a friend of the Jesuruns — Brakel even risked ministerial displeasure by daringly stating: "The information Your Excellency received on the Jesurun House is very one-sided." He also completely disagreed with P. van der Does de Willebois (in Venezuelan sources called Villebois), the new Dutch Foreign Minister, with regard to the pending trial of Mr. Worm and the Midas crew, considered by The Hague as a mock trial.[23] If it was this new Foreign Minister's idea to send a squadron to the Caribbean, it was his first blunder, which compounded previous errors in judgment of the Venezuelan Question.[24]

Guzmán Blanco had braced himself. The day before the supposed arrival of the Dutch naval force he had sent his artillerists and their finest British cannons to La Guaira followed by 1,000 men of the Guardia. When the three Dutch men-of-war arrived — officially on a courtesy visit — they were anchored, on orders of the president, at a roadstead just opposite a land battery of 20 pieces. At both sides of this fortification were private houses, shops, and warehouses, many belonging to English, Dutch, and German merchants. Even the aggressive commander of the squadron realized the impossibility of silencing that battery without causing tremendous damage to the neighborhood.[25]

A highly emotional discussion between the commander, Brakel, and the three captains of the men-of-war followed. The conclusion was a victory for Brakel's persuasiveness and Guzmán Blanco's astute strategy. No force would be used. The commander would not even pay a courtesy visit to Caracas, although his crews were granted shore leave. The squadron left March 12 after a visit of barely two days. Seldom had a well-publicized expedition accomplished so little.

A less bleak note for the Dutch will finish this chapter. At the end of March, the captain, crew, and passenger of the *Midas* unexpectedly arrived at Curaçao on the English steamer *Atlas,* the mysterious Waldemar Worm being the first to disembark.[26] This promptly raised high hopes that existing tensions could be reduced and cordial relations reestablished.

11. THE CRISIS OF 1875

Beneath the apparent tranquility following the humiliating departure of the Dutch squadron, another crisis was already developing. On March 20, 1875 Venezuelan Foreign Minister Blanco informed Brakel of what he called "a new conspiracy". A continuous stream of defeated Coro rebels had gathered at Curaçao and more were flocking there daily. Their leaders were putting the shattered organisation back into working order.[1]

On orders from Caracas, the new commercial agent of the republic, W. E. Boye, successor of the hapless Mendes, pressed strongly for cooperation and pointed out to the Dutch governor those refugees who were to be expelled: General León Colina and his son Manuel, and the generals Fernando Adames and Eusebio Díaz. Stressing the subversive activities of these men, Boye, in collaboration with Blanco laced the demands with blunt threats.[2] Determined to obtain Dutch compliance and at the same time to punish the uncooperative coastal population of the republic, Guzmán Blanco reimposed the blockade of Coro and Maracaibo lifted shortly before. As Wagner was quick to realize, this act not only punished the merchants of those towns but dealt also a damaging blow to the Dutch island's trade. Curaçao derived its limited prosperity from the transit trade with those regions; once it lost it, the governor feared, commerce would move to other places and never return.[3]

On August 16, while both Wagner and Brakel pondered this development, the Second Chamber of the Dutch States General discussed the Venezuelan Question. The crew of the *Midas* had petitioned Parliament for relief, and discussions on their request constituted an important detail of the Chamber's agenda. Although the Dutch press sided almost unanimously with the crew, it was restrained in its comments and did not dramatize the issue. An exception must be made for the *Dagblad van Zuid-Holland en 's-Gravenhage* (Daily Paper of South-Holland and The Hague) which professed a pro-Venezuelan point of view in several articles signed by Hugo Sassen, a nephew of the former Attorney General of Curaçao, who had had difficulties with Wagner, resulting in his dismissal. The close tie between Hugo Sassen and the *Opinión Nacional* is highly suggestive of the aggressive nature of this young Dutchman. The *Opinión Nacional* published one of his articles entitled "Venezuela y Holanda" (Venezuela and Holland) with a stirring commentary, thus adding fuel to the fire.[4] The article itself pointedly reminded the reader of the high respect the Curaçao population had for the Guzmán Blanco regime, although a handful of greedy merchants created confusion and favored civil disorders in the republic which promoted their sales of war materiel. The article harshly critized the governor of the island and concluded by suggesting the prohibition of war materiel imports into the colony with the exception of strictly local needs.

The continuing strained relations produced a certain rapprochement between the Dutch chargé d'affaires and the Governor of Curaçao. Both realized the time had come to stop accusing each other at the expense of the Dutch cause. Brakel's pro-Venezuelan feelings cooled considerably after the squadron's obvious frustration, while the endless demands of Caracas, combined with open threats, generated to some extent Brakel's understanding of Wagner's attitude. The accumulation of Blanco's notes on Brakel's desk, always adding more names to the list of people he wanted removed from the island,[5] began to have an adverse effect on the Dutch chargé d'affaires. Guzmán Blanco's aggressiveness did not encourage any effort toward reconciliation. In his message to Congress of May 5, 1875, the president stated that "we would not have incurred the considerable expenses nor the great sacrifices required by the last campaign, nor would the country have suffered the enormous losses which it deplores now" if there had not been support for the Coro revolt from Curaçao. He then announced his formal protest to the Dutch government concerning the financial damages caused by the late rebellion. "I ordered," he said, "the booking of a special account of war expenses with the intention of requesting a refund as one of the consequences which resulted from this conduct of colonial agents." [6]

Bypassing Brakel, who was fully empowered to conduct negotiations, Guzmán Blanco addressed himself directly to The Hague in a long letter which with intensified anger outlined his complaints concerning problems of contraband and losses — up to 50 per cent, he claimed — for the Venezuelan treasury. The note tried to prove that administrative disorder would never end as long as this trade continued, provoking the government's discredit in the interior and the irreparable ruin of all creditors. There would be no remedy to this depressing situation but to stop the clandestine trade of a few unscrupulous speculators on the island of Curaçao.[7]

This was only an introduction to his major demands. The Venezuelan government first requested a pecuniary indemnity for losses suffered during the Coro insurrection and second, it underscored the political necessity of recalling the Governor of Curaçao, "the main contributor to the disgrace and massacre of Venezuelans by his efforts to frustrate all Venezuelan demands." The indemnity bill of 4,250,000 guilders did not yet represent the full amount. With the customary threats of differential duties and closure of the ports of Coro and Maracaibo, he outlined his strategy in case of refusal, "Venezuela had to be protected against cruel Curaçao." [8]

Guzmán Blanco's note was delivered to The Hague by a special ambassador extraordinary and minister plenipotenciary, José María de Rojas.[9] The Venezuelan government, increasingly concentrating on a new approach and dissatisfied by evasive and vague answers from Brakel, avoided regular diplomatic channels in an effort to deal directly with its adversary. The Dutch chargé d'affaires knew about this mission soon enough although official information came much later.[10] Incredible as it may seem, he did not inform The Hague.

Secrecy is often the key to success. Guzmán Blanco wanted Rojas to be accredited to the Netherlands before Brakel knew about it and could notify his government.[11] The Venezuelan diplomat hurried off to Europe and received his final instructions via the Venezuelan consuls of St. Nazaire and Paris.[12] Together with his secretary, Antonio Parra Bolívar, Venezuelan consul in Le Havre, he arrived in The Hague on June 1, 1875. There he met the Marquis de Arcícollar, Spanish minister resident to the Netherlands, who was of great help to Rojas, who had neither friends nor acquaintances in The Hague.[13]

As a defense mechanism, understandable in all circumstances but more so with a president of excessive arrogance and limited patience, the Venezuelan minister plenipotentiary and ambassador extraordinary made himself both in his autobiography *Recuerdos de la Patria* (Memories of the Fatherland) and in his correspondence with Blanco very much the hero in his meetings with Dutch Foreign Minister Van der Does de Willebois, despite the fact that he must soon have concluded that his special mission was failing miserably. Van der Does, a man of the old school of traditional diplomacy which regarded the rules of the game as important as the game itself, had misgivings about the status of the new envoy. Pulido, the previous ambassador, was never officially recalled and consequently still functioned formally as Venezuela's representative, although he resided in Paris. Brakel, on the other hand, had full authority to handle existing questions.[14] The first complication was soon solved by Pulido's resignation,[15] while Van der Does — maintaining that he read about Rojas' mission for the first time in the Dutch daily papers — realized the existing difficulties between the two nations and especially the interests of Curaçao's merchant elite could not tolerate too fussy an attitude. Hopefully the mission of the new Venezuelan agent, he informed the King, "would offer an opportunity to solve the tensions between the two nations." [16]

Thus Rojas achieved a small initial success which gave him immense personal satisfaction. King William III declared himself willing to receive the new ambassador, which meant he officially accepted Rojas as the representative of his country.[17] The solemn audience took place on June 16, 1875.[18] Two days later the haggling with Van der Does began.

It opened with a curious incident. Rojas handed the Dutch Foreign Minister his government's long note accompanied by an impressive package of documentary proof — testimonials of eye-witnesses, for instance — plus an account of expenses caused by the latest revolt. All these documents were written in Spanish. Not only was the Dutch Foreign Minister unable to read them but, incredible as it may sound, it soon appeared that no one in the Dutch Foreign Office was able to translate them. They had to go to an outside translator. This embarrassing situation caused some delay.[19]

The postponement was unintentional although Rojas suspected otherwise. To solve the temporary impasse, Van der Does asked Rojas to summarize the contents. This resume, written in French, was handed in three days later.[20] The two demands — indemnity for expenses and the recall of Wagner — caught Van der Does off-guard. He immediately informed the Cabinet and the King of what was going on.[21]

The importance of the matter required two full sessions of the Cabinet and the following decisions were made:

The Dutch Foreign Minister will not enter into negotiations with the Venezuelan envoy until
a. the schooner *Midas* is returned, and
b. the ports of Coro and Maracaibo are reopened.[22]

To stress the peace-loving intentions of the Netherlands the port of Curaçao would be closed to the export of war materiel, pending the deliberation on the Dutch prerequisites for negotiations. The Dutch government solemnly declared that Curaçao would resume its normal condition of free port if its demands were not satisfied by October 1. It also reserved for itself the right to discuss the demand for indemnity by the Venezuelan government until the Dutch demands were satisfied.[23]

These decisions of the Dutch Cabinet were neither examples of farsightedness nor of tactful diplomatic maneuvering. True, the Venezuelan demands were worded offensively, but the Dutch note handed to Rojas was even more clumsily formulated and provocative. The fact that a time limit was added made it look very much like an ultimatum. Ill-conceived and reflecting no insight into the mind and character of the Illustrious American or the awakening Venezuelan national consciousness, it increased popular agitation, already sensitized by the Yellow press. Rojas himself professed "the most profound amazement in taking cognizance of such an exceptionally serious decision." [24]

The consequences of the Dutch note were not foreseen by Van der Does. Tensions now rose to the level of an open conflict. Rojas, stupefied, but clearly understanding the vital importance of the next step, dared not move on his own and asked his government for instructions.[25] This meant two months' respite.

The apprehension manifested by the Venezuelan envoy was not yet shared by the Dutch Foreign Minister. He optimistically informed Brakel of recent developments, ordering him to bring the two demands of the Dutch government to the attention of Venezuelan authorities. This involved Brakel in the negotiations and clearly showed the determination of the Dutch Cabinet not to bypass him. Warned of the undiplomatic treatment he could expect from the Venezuelans "which one does not have to fear from civilized nations," he was further cautioned that "if you have well-founded concern for serious complications regarding your dignity, you should depart and take leave in Curaçao." Van der Does probably envisioned a humiliating experience similar to Rolandus's. Fear of such a treatment was reflected in The Hague's advice to take deposited payments on the claims to a safe place.[26]

As mentioned before, Brakel had known about Rojas' mision in May, 1875, when Guzmán Blanco opened the Venezuelan Congress, but had not informed Van der Does. Officially informed at the end of June, Brakel's notification came too late to warn the Dutch Foreign Minister in time. The reason for bypassing Brakel, Blanco explained, was the anti-Dutch mood of the Venezuelan capital.[27] Rojas' appointment was never announced in the Gaceta Oficial.

Belatedly Brakel sent Van der Does information on Rojas. The latter had been a partner in a family enterprise and later established a business relationship with the well-known commercial house of H. L. Boulton & Company in Caracas. He had accompanied Guzmán Blanco to London when the rising *caudillo* arranged the famous loan for his country which laid the foundation of his considerable wealth. In 1874 Rojas prepared a settlement of Spanish claims in which Guzmán Blanco himself was to become later the most significant claimant. Rojas then tried to repeat this with the British keepers of Venezuelan debentures, but this effort was indignantly rebuffed by Queen Victoria's government.[28]

At the time of Rojas' arrival in The Hague, General Colina published a ringing manifesto in Curaçao addressed to the Venezuelan National Congress and his countrymen, calling them to armed resistance against the "oppressive regime" of Guzmán Blanco.[29] Subsequent articles in Curaçao's *El Imparcial* doubled Venezuelan anger.[30] In a way these irritations were counterbalanced by the *Gaceta Internacional,* which sympathetically reviewed Venezuelan complaints against the colonial government of Curaçao and bluntly suggested the distribution of "letters of marque" in case the Dutch resorted to armed intervention.[31] Presumably written by Hugo Sassen, they repeated the battle cry of the former Attorney General, his uncle: "Recall Wagner." Both Sassens saw the Governor of Curaçao as the main impediment to good relations with Venezuela.[32]

Curiously enough, around that same time an apparently serious effort toward reconciliation between the two main actors in this Caribbean drama was unfolding behind the scenes. Abraham J. Jesurun paid a visit to Caracas around the middle of July.[33] A certain Olavarría seemed to have been the promotor of his unexpected rapprochement with Guzmán Blanco. The latter received his long-time antagonist courteously and showed some goodwill by returning the *Julieta* and its crew,[34] but no immediate agreement was reached, although the "Caribbean Rothschild" must have been quite willing to make concessions. Jesurun returned to Curaçao in August,[35] but six weeks later he turned up again in Caracas. This time the two concluded an agreement.[36] But before it could go into effect, the demands of Van der Does caused a popular uproar in the Venezuelan capital.

The unlikely alliance of old rivals amidst the manifestations of popular indignance and anti-Dutch sentiment was not so strange as it might appear at first sight. They needed each other, each for his own particular reasons and private interests. Guzmán Blanco was willing to recognize some doubtful claims, expressed in the protocol of December 27, 1867, although the interest rate of 15 per cent had to be reduced to 9. Jesurun was willing to renounce diplomatic support for some reclamations dated after April 27, 1870. For the moment the protracted feud was over. Ingeniously Guzmán Blanco had brought one of his most stubborn enemies into his camp. An immediate result, in spite of the popular and official uproar caused by the Yellow press, was the continuation of payments.[37]

This reconciliation was strengthened with the expulsion of General León Colina. Although it is not sure whether Jesurun's desertion from his cause influenced Wagner, the general's close association with Venezuelan upheavals suddenly became too obvious to ignore.[38] This expulsion was soon followed by that of Riera who, in the words of the Dutch Foreign Minister, "had violated the limits of hospitality and decency . . . in regard to the heads of foreign governments." [39]

But these promising indications of rapprochement instantly evaporated when Rojas' letter arrived, informing his government of the Dutch position. Brakel was deeply impressed by the capital's reaction and the sudden uproar of national indignation which surrounded him. Blanco uttered stronger threats, but he was only a puppet. The real minister of foreign affairs was Antonio Leocadio Guzmán, the president's father and, in Brakel's evaluation "the most capable and shrewdest statesman of the republic." [40] The elder Guzmán now launched an effective anti-Dutch campaign, agitating for national unity behind the Great Liberal against the foreign aggressor.

By this time the Dutch Foreign Minister Van der Does had recovered somewhat from the political myopia demonstrated by his notes to Rojas and Brakel. His present position seemed far from strong or enviable. The Dutch democratic governmental system made Cabinet members responsible to the people's representatives in both chambers of Parliament. He faced interpellations in the Second Chamber and a growing uneasiness in the Dutch press, which understood the possibly fatal consequences of the political impasse. The chargé d'affaires in Caracas seemed to offer an acceptable scapegoat. At the end of August, when Rojas' communication on the same item had just caused the first consternation, he had received Van der Does' instructions of July 27 with the Dutch demands. Wisely he had waited a few days to give the Venezuelans time to cool off before informing Blanco. To blame the disturbed Brakel for the sudden crisis, accusing him of not understanding instructions, was not only cowardly but also contrary to the facts. Caracas was already dramatically aroused by Rojas' account of diplomatic happenings in The Hague. The Dutch Foreign Minister ignored this. "I see with regret," he wrote, "that you misunderstood my orders." His eagerness to save his own skin did not include much regard for the truth. The ominous deadline he had set was no longer mentioned.

"Before entering into negotiations with the Venezuelan government on pretended wrongs we desired first and foremost to have its hostile measures recalled, i.e., the return of the *Midas* and the opening of the closed ports ... I am truly amazed that you acted in such a way as if transfer of negotiations to Caracas was feasible."

Of course a transfer of negotiations, which had been suggested by Brakel, was not the point; the demand to open the two closed ports within a set time limit was. Did Van der Does willingly ignore this? Whatever the case, Brakel was informed that at the end of October another Dutch naval force would be sent to the West.[41] This unfortunate decision of the Dutch Cabinet exemplifies The Hague's diplomatic ignorance. Dutch diplomacy had lost touch with West Indian realities.

At the beginning of October, Rojas, still waiting for Guzmán Blanco's response to the Dutch demands, complained about some articles in the Dutch press on the alleged mistreatment of the captain and crew of the *Midas* in La Rotunda, the Caracas prison. The whole affair, Rojas protested, had "resulted in public outrage". He called it "wrong and little to the advantage of his government and his country". He categorically denied any accusation of wrongdoing. The Curaçao Committee, he contended, was its source and he defined its members sarcastically as a group of "wicked Dutch speculators working against peace in Venezuela".[42]

But this attitude soon stiffened when the answer arrived on the Dutch counterdemands. Guzmán Blanco was willing to return the *Midas* it said, not as an admission of guilt, because the seizure was "legally judged and condemned by tribunals of the republic",[43] but as proof to The Hague and the world of a sincere desire to create an atmosphere of friendship and conciliation.

The second part of the Venezuelan note was less conciliatory. Regarding the opening or closing of the national ports, any demand by a foreign government could never be accepted. It bluntly stated that this would mean a "renunciation of national jurisdiction over national territory, abdication of sovereignty of Venezuela, and treason to national independence."

Rojas handed this note to the Dutch Foreign Minister on October 6, exactly one month after it was sent. Accompanying it was a new litany of complaints which, although irritating, did not essentially aggravate the situation. However, Caracas now fell into the same trap which Van der Does had not avoided. It added a time limit to its threat to break relations if the Dutch insisted on their second demand, the re-opening of the closed ports as a preamble to negotiations on reclamations for indemnities. This time limit of three days, as in the case of the Dutch demands, had all the menacing characteristics of an ultimatum.

The Venezuelan demand created resentment and a pronounced anti-Venezuelan feeling. Van der Does, more confident because of this encouraging sign, now insisted on the reopening of the closed ports of Coro and Maracaibo before he would be willing to open any discussion.

"Your government, Monsieur le Ministre," he wrote Rojas, "has not studied the problem from the right angle ... The Venezuelan government, of its own free will, closed two of its most important ports to stop communication with Curaçao. At the same time, however, it asks us, for its exclusive advantage, to keep our port of Curaçao closed to the export of war materiel."

Regarding the requested indemnity Van der Does wrote:

"You ask a pecuniary indemnity as a reparation of your grievances, which means, ultimately, that we have not closed our port hermetically enough. In the face of these demands, His Majesty's government cannot admit discussion of even one claim in reparation of grievances which your government wishes to have evaluated, as long as the ports of Venezuela are closed to Dutch trade." [44]

The thrust of Van der Does's analysis was lost. Events moved rapidly towards the ominous deadline of October 9 set by the Venezuelan government. At that time Rojas informed the Dutch Foreign Minister that, not having received a satisfactory answer, he considered the diplomatic relations between the two countries broken and blamed the Dutch government for imposing upon Venezuela a demand morally impossible to satisfy.[45]

The King was immediately informed of this break. A cable was sent — via St. Thomas — ordering Brakel to ask for his passport and to leave Venezuela for Curaçao. Meanwhile, diplomatic representation was arranged through the minister of the German Empire, Dr. Erwin Stammann. Brakel was also ordered to take the legation archives with him or to seal them and hand them over to one of his colleagues.[46] Wagner was informed.[47]

A squadron composed of three men-of-war prepared to sail for Curaçao to reinforce the one man-of-war stationed at the island. The Dutch moved vigorously to protect their overseas dependencies and their interests. The Venezuelans, incensed and offended, united behind their arrogant master.

12. THE THREAT OF WAR

In a democratically ruled nation — and the Netherlands could be considered as such — where ministerial responsibility was an effective brake on executive power abuses, an incident as serious as the severance of diplomatic relations had to be explained to the people's representatives. Consequently a member of the Second Chamber of the States General acted promptly by asking the Foreign Minister for complete information. On October 11, 1875, an unhappy Van der Does faced the members of this Chamber with a long weak speech in which he defended his position.[1] It was followed by long debates which revealed strong concern over recent developments in the West.

As the immediate cause of the present conflicts the minister rightly named the *Midas* question and the Coro revolt. While belittling the role of Curaçao and its merchants, he summarized to the Chamber the Venezuelan demands: indemnity for expenses caused by the Coro revolution, replacement of the Governor of Curaçao, expulsion of a number of Venezuelan refugees, the closing of the Curaçao port to the export of war materiel, and censorship of Curaçao's offensive press.

As he was unable to understand the root of the conflict — the poorly regulated trade in war materiel — the Dutch Foreign Minister declared openly that he was not willing to discuss these points until Venezuela returned the *Midas* and reopened the ports of Coro and Maracaibo to Curaçao's trade. "I would then be prepared," he declared, "to confer with the Venezuelan envoy about his demands," [2] a dangerous statement rightly interpreted by Rojas as a *de jure* recognition of Venezuela's right to indemnity.[3] Most of his speech contained the usual diplomatic rhetoric. "We share," he concluded, "the wish of the Venezuelan envoy that the difficulties between our countries may be solved in a peaceful and mutually satisfactory manner."

Such words were certainly not the popular vocabulary of the Venezuelan press. Its vitriolic articles surpassed by far those of the island press, *El Imparcial* and the *Civilisadó,* and provided to no small degree more raw material for an aggravation of the situation. "*Por fin se acerca la hora de la revindicación de Venezuela,*" and "*Dios tarda pero no olvida,*" for instance, were some headlines under which the *Diario de Avisos* kept tensions alive. Similar heated discharges appeared in the *Opinión Nacional,* inspired by official encouragement.[4]

A cooler evaluation of the conflict was provided by the Dutch consul at Le Havre, P. van Bunge, a close friend of Parra Bolívar, Rojas's secretary.

> "The Dutch government," he wrote to the Ambassador of the Netherlands in Paris, "loses sight of the fact that the present President of the Republic, Guzmán Blanco, is a very energetic man who will not shrink from anything to end what he considers to be the nuisance of Curaçao... He should be taken seriously. He certainly is able and willing to carry out his threats and to issue, for instance, "letters of marque" to hinder Dutch shipping and stop smuggling." [5]

From his conversations with Parra Bolívar he knew that the Venezuelan government was quite willing to compromise and perhaps even give up its indemnity claims in return for the assurance that the Dutch would not insist on a reopening of the closed ports. This, the Dutch consul argued, "could well be a basis for new negotiations." [6] Possibly for this reason Rojas had been ordered by his government to stay in Paris. But Van Bunge added a warning: "In the opposite case the Guzmán Blanco government will not hesitate to declare war." Big American capitalists and "followers of the Monroe Doctrine", the Dutch consul asserted, "seem to have advanced huge sums to Venezuela and the "letters of marque" really appear to be for the North Americans." [7]

Indeed, it may well be that public opinion in the United States was indifferent to this minor Caribbean conflict — only a small ripple in the high tide of American and British imperialism — but astute American businessmen with a keen eye for profits were fully aware of its implications and were extremely interested bystanders. The Dutch Foreign Minister, far from underrating their interest, entertained real fears that they would buy permits for privateering as soon as Guzmán Blanco initiated their sale, and he imagined the Caribbean swarming with modern buccaneers. His serious efforts to convince the French and British governments of this possibility manifested these fears.[8]

They had indeed some grounds. Rojas, while in Paris, was ordered to make contact with weapon merchants and sea captains and was supplied with blank "letters of marque". The old pirate spirit of earlier centuries seems to have been affected by the mercantile tendencies of the age; contacts requested a deposit of 50,000 French francs, which Caracas refused.[9]

The role played by the newly-born German Empire in this conflict dramatized the stiff competition between great powers in world affairs. In a meeting with the Dutch envoy W. F. Rochussen, the German Foreign Minister Von Bülow asked with German bonhomie if it were true that certain difficulties had developed between The Hague and Curaçao. This question, which greatly disturbed the envoy, must be seen against the background of persistent rumors that Germany had her eyes on a Caribbean naval base. The recent reconciliation between Jesurun and Guzmán Blanco added a new dimension to this picture. The eldest partner of the firm, Abraham J. Jesurun, had been consul general of the North German Confederation in Curaçao since 1868 and of the German Empire since 1871. If the Germans indeed had plans for a Caribbean naval base, the possibility that Jesurun would become the middle man between Berlin and The Hague in case of a Curaçao revolt added to the Dutch Foreign Minister's worries.[10]

Consequently, the Dutch did not trust the Germans any more than the British. But probably, the chargé d'affaires in Caracas was blessedly unaware of this complication. When he hurriedly left the Venezuelan capital on October 22, he consigned the Dutch interests in the republic to the last man he was expected to choose: Erwin Stammann, the minister of the German Empire. The latter also took care of the sealed legation archives.[11] The new function provided Stammann with a Great German feeling: he now had responsibility for Dutch subjects in Venezuela together with the payments of the Venezuelan government to Dutch claimants of "diplomatic debts".

Stammann seems to have been an able and honest diplomat. He succeeded in convincing Caracas to continue the payments in spite of the suspension of relations. Guzmán Blanco did not object. As this attitude led Stammann to believe that the Venezuelans were willing to compromise, he instantly took a further step in offering his mediation in the conflict. The Hague viewed this request with certain apprehension. The envoy could have been encouraged by Von Bülow. The latter had discussed the Venezuelan-Dutch difficulties with Martín J. Sanabria, former exile in Curaçao, expelled with the Guzmans in 1870, and now Venezuelan envoy in Berlin. Perhaps Von Bülow saw for himself a role as the founder of a German West Indian empire. The irritating problems Germany had had with Venezuela were still fresh in his mind.

In those days the trade of Maracaibo was almost exclusively in the hands of German merchants, who complained angrily about their huge losses resulting from Guzmán Blanco's measures.[12]

The upsurge of German interest in the West was not the only cause of Dutch uneasiness. At the same time a Venezuelan agent was visiting the United States buying Remington rifles and heavy artillery, and there was an uncomfirmed rumor that Guzmán Blanco was trying to buy two or three monitors. The Dutch envoy in Washington was ordered to request official American disapproval of such sales.[13] The interlocking nature of this information caused no slight agitation to the Dutch Foreign Minister, but his fears did not materialize. Soon he received the relieving news that the United States had no men-of-war for sale. Some worry still kept him awake. "If I could but know that public opinion in the United States is on our side," he wrote the envoy in Washington. "Our problems with Venezuela have not yet attracted much attention," answered the latter truthfully.[14] Then came the disturbing news that Venezuela had tried to buy machine guns in France.[15]

Meanwhile the October 1 deadline had arrived and Wagner, never a champion of a soft line policy toward Venezuela, coolly ignored rumors and opened Curaçao's port to the export of war materiel as instructed by the Minister for the Colonies. Within a week, however, he received orders from a confused Minister to suspend export. The port had been open for five days. No war materiel had left the island in that short period.

Brakel had left Caracas on October 22, 1875, three days after Blanco had informed him of the break in relations. A Dutch man-of-war sent by Governor Wagner had picked him up at La Guaira and brought him to Curaçao. In the more relaxed atmosphere of the island, Wagner and Brakel discussed the tense state of affairs. The possibility of a Venezuelan invasion was weighed and discarded. It was clear that the republic, without a merchant marine, and with only three or four coast guard vessels, could not muster enough tonnage for such a risky enterprise. Other rumors were easier to believe. According to them, Guzmán Blanco had bought lead and gunpowder in St. Thomas worth 16,000 *venezolanos* and would call 30,000 to 40,000 men to arms.[16] That he was preparing for a fight was known even before the diplomatic break. Blanco had repeatedly urged Rojas to stall for time to strengthen the coastal defense, especially the ports of La Guaira and Puerto Cabello, as the threat of a Dutch attack was taken quite seriously.[17] Specific instructions for the port defenses were sent out immediately after the diplomatic break became known.[18]

In the meantime, the Dutch in Curaçao waited anxiously for the arrival of the new squadron. Three men-of-war had left the Netherlands for Curaçao at the beginning of November. Although Venezuela had expressed her willingness to give back the *Midas,* the ship had not yet been returned. Consequently, the commander's instructions included an order to seize the *Midas* wherever he might find her. This order was later canceled.[19]

Thus both parties faced a complex set of difficulties. Antagonism and irritation were spinning them between war and peace, although neither was inclined toward the use of force. The *New York Tribune* appraised the situation aptly: "It is obvious from the explanation of the Dutch Foreign Minister that war is not apprehended with Venezuela although diplomatic relations with that country have been suspended." The situation was compared to that between Mexico and Great Britain, as these two nations had had no official relations since the Emperor Maximilian's execution, although they for all practical purposes remained on good terms.[20]

The news of another approaching Dutch naval force stirred up more bad blood among the Venezuelans and generated vituperative articles in their press.[21] Very harmful to the Dutch cause was Brakel's lack of alertness. While in Caracas he had not obtained much information on Venezuelan naval and military strength. "I had expected from you as a former soldier," the Dutch Foreign Minister wrote, "extensive and trustworthy information on Venezuela's means of defense, and on the strength of her armed forces." [22]

However, few incidents occurred. With the news that relations were broken, a mob plundered the Dutch schooner *Julieta* (owner unknown) in Puerto Cabello.[23] The Dutch brick *Arcadië* had dropped anchor in the port of Barcelona, unaware of the diplomatic crisis, and was forbidden to depart. Stammann's intervention, however, resulted in the release of the ship.[24]

In appraising Brakel's performance as chargé d'affaires, the conclusion becomes obvious that he failed in his mission. He may have had a more pleasant personality than his predecessor Rolandus, as confirmed by his temporary popularity in Caracas' diplomatic and *guzmancista* circles, but his shortcomings as a diplomat were not balanced by personal affability.

He might have successfully concluded the negotiations on the "diplomatic debts", but he did so at the expense of the Jesurun House, which had to drop 50 per cent of its claims. Worse was his impermissible failure to warn Wagner of the outbreak of the Coro revolt which had such serious consequences. Wagner received notice approximately ten days after the rebellion started and in the meantime the *Midas* had departed. Nor did he inform the Dutch Foreign Minister of Rojas's mission, although he had known about it for nearly two months before being officially informed. These two omissions find small compensation in his news of the Jesurun-Guzmán Blanco reconciliation. His failure to report adequately on Venezuelan military preparedness was also an unforgivable lapse, the more incomprehensible because he was a soldier by profession. At the bottom of all these blunders, however, was his complete lack of psychological insight into the nature of the Illustrious American and an absolute failure to understand the Venezuelan national character. But he was not the only one to blame. He was nominated for the Caracas post by Van der Does' predecessor, Gericke van Herwijnen, who thus indirectly shares the burden for this mission's failure.[25]

13. THE FATEFUL YEAR 1876

For many years a state of "interrupted official relations" characterized the position of the Netherlands with regard to Guzmán Blanco's Venezuela. During those years the usual irritations decreased visibly and had less and less impact on basic attitudes. Both sides made some weak efforts to penetrate the wall of misunderstandings that separated them, but that objective was not achieved until eighteen years later. Rojas' analysis, made six months after his departure from The Hague that "all pending questions between the Netherlands and Venezuela have been solved" was based more on optimism than on sound judgment.[1]

Nothing was solved for a long time. The interruption of normal relations was gradually accepted as a nuisance with which the inhabitants of both the republic and Curaçao had to cope. This unnatural situation hardened into a routine of which outbursts of Venezuelan nationalism formed part and whereby the Dutch argument for the use of force came to be habitually overruled. The very noisy presses of both Venezuela and Curaçao continued to voice their opinions with little official restraint. The fulminations of the "deserter" Henríquez in *El Imparcial* matched those of the *Opinión Nacional,* while the Venezuelan point of view found a strong spokesman in the *Revista Hispano Americana,* printed in Brussels and circulated throughout Europe. The Venezuelan cause also received aid from several articles in the *Gaceta Internacional.* Rojas rendered some service with his pamphlet *Het Nederlandsch Venezolaansch Conflict* (The Dutch Venezuelan Conflict), published under the pseudonym Amigo de las Antillas. On a more scholarly level were the comments of the internationally-known lawyer, G. Rolin Jacquemijns, in his excellent exposition of the conflict in the *Revue du Droit International.*[2]

With the shift from active confrontation to a kind of "cold war" the diplomatic moves indicated an increasing gulf between the two nations. The Venezuelan government countered Wagner's brief suspension of the Royal Degree on October 1, 1875, by permitting only ships under special orders to sail from its ports to Curaçao. Despite British complaints, the Guzmán Blanco regime exerted pressure to force foreign ships to avoid the island.[3] The merchants of the two closed ports, especially the Germans in Maracaibo, voiced their displeasure loudly. However, they never generated enough popular indignation to have the ports reopened. The Caracas government did not heed their cries and the capital's merchants were only too pleased with the elimination of dangerous competitors. At the end of December, the government restricted coastal shipping exclusively to vessels under the Venezuelan flag. This ended practically all foreign navigation along the coast and constituted another blow to Curaçao, while at the same time a rise in import duties hurt also the island's trade.[4]

Wagner did his utmost not to irritate Guzmán Blanco. After hearing of the severance of relations, general Colina returned to the island expecting a hearty welcome. He was greatly disappointed when he was told to leave again.[5] Wagner also tried to blunt the impact of the greatest irritant, the Dutch squadron, which arrived in the Caribbean at the beginning of 1876. From the outset, the reinforcement of Dutch naval power so close to the Venezuelan coast angered the latter country. In his message to Congress of April 5, 1876, Guzmán Blanco discussed the Dutch "threat" at great length, and although his emotional rhetoric was purposefully exaggerated, there was no doubt of his sincerity: "The display of this squadron ... together with a threatening and insulting press could become dangerous," he said, "if by intimidation we should open our ports."

Dutch intimidation would fail, maintained the Venezuelan President. He noted pointedly that he had the support of his people, and that even if that were not the case, Venezuelans would not hesitate to defend their fatherland against foreign invasion. "As for me," he argued, "I would like and I will try to procure peace without any condition except that there will be no discussion of the opening of our ports, because that would put into question our sovereign right of independence." The Dutch claims, he told his audience, would be paid regardless of the present stagnation.[6]

There was no immediate Dutch reaction to this message. The King conventionally repeated in his Speech of September 20, 1875 (before the break of relations) that relations with foreign powers continued to be of a "very friendly character". He admitted, however, that Curaçao's trade had experienced some problems resulting from the civil unrest in Venezuela.[7] A year later, the threat of armed confrontation forced the recognition of the existence of problems. The King hoped "that the complications with Venezuela will soon find their solution; this will certainly benefit Curaçao." The Second Chamber added "We share with Your Majesty the hope that the difficulties in the trade of Curaçao can be solved by negotiations."

In several meetings the Dutch Cabinet debated the Venezuelan Question at some length and severely criticized the Foreign Minister. While no miraculous solutions were found one important item disappeared almost imperceptibly from the discussions: the demand for the reopening of the ports of Coro and Maracaibo.[9]

Guzmán Blanco himself made an important move towards future reconciliation by separating the offices of diplomatic representative and consular agent. This eliminated conflicts between the duties of the consul as his countrymen's solicitor and of the diplomat as his nation's representative.[10] The importance of this decision was evident: it kept channels of communication open. Dutch consuls continued to function along the Venezuelan coast in spite of the political disruption.

Growing optimism caused by this decision, however, was dampened by another one concerning the diplomatic debts. It was a minor matter, but the fact that Guzmán Blanco acted unilaterally prompted strong protests. In July the British government approached the Dutch regarding a joint diplomatic action against the republic.[11] The Dutch Foreign Office followed the cautious course of not trusting Great Britain just as it had not trusted Germany previously. It alerted the Governor of Curaçao to discover the reaction of the Curaçao claimants to Guzmán Blanco's changes.[12] This prudent behavior probably continued after Stammann's meeting with Guzmán Blanco. During their talks the Venezuelan president explained his reasons for changing the claims agreement before his term of office expired on February 20, 1877. Pardo's widow who lived in Caracas, answered Stammann's questionnaire favorably; the German Minister had to approach the other two, Jesurun and Senior, through Wagner.[13] After a delay caused by red tape, both agreed to accept the new arrangement but only if all foreign creditors involved consented to it. Deeply distrustful of the government's financial transactions, they requested that the claimants' own legation serve as banks where the payments would be deposited. "I am thus not able to give the Venezuelan government a definite answer," wrote Stammann, "and I regret this in view of the interests trusted to me." [14] At that time the claims of the Jesurun House amounted to 368,211 *venezolanos,* those of Senior to almost 33,000 and of Pardo to 44,000.[15]

Of course a collective action of all creditor countries involved would have been impossible. Stammann came to this conclusion after his discussions with the respective envoys in Caracas.[16] "It is understandable," he wrote, "that some nations cannot accept the new arrangement if one looks at the arbitrary distribution of money." But others could.

The distribution was as follows:

	venezolanos	venezolanos monthly
Spain received against a claim of	1,400,000	2,796
U.S.	1,100,000	2,796
Denmark	14,000	305
England	190,000	2,204
France	1,430,000	5,655
The Netherlands (Curaçao)	440,000	1,444

Most monthly payments would be less than the ones agreed upon in 1873. Guzmán Blanco knew this. But he also knew that there was not much the claimants could do about it. As his new Foreign Minister, Canuto García pointed out, the new arrangement was an act of Congress (of May, 1876) and only Congress could change it. He admitted, however, that the president had the constitutional right to direct diplomatic negotiations on this matter.[17] For the time being this ended the debate.

A new platform for diplomatic discussions on the Venezuelan-Dutch conflict seemed possible when the Venezuelan envoy in Washington, Juan B. Dalla Costa, openly sought Secretary of State Hamilton Fish's mediation with the Dutch.[18] Fish was not reluctant to play a peacemaker's role similar to that of Poinsett in Chile. Encouraged, Dalla Costa then contacted the Dutch minister in Washington, Von Pestel, and proudly cited Guzmán Blanco's authorization. But he outraged the envoy with some undiplomatic outbursts about the "menace to peace and amity" of the Dutch squadron in Curaçao.[19] The Dutch daily press was not very helpful either and saw the possible mediation of the United States as a Venezuelan attempt to take over Curaçao.[20] The Spanish ambassador in Rome further alarmed the Dutch Foreign Office with the rumor that in any conflict provoked by the Dutch, the United States would side with Venezuela.[21]

The Dutch noted the American attitude with an unhappy awareness of the U.S. pretensions in the Caribbean and this nation's power. Uneasiness prevailed when James Birney, American Minister to The Hague, approached the Dutch Foreign Minister about the chances of a reconciliation. A long note exposed his country's unselfish interest in the conflict and asked the following questions:

1. Were the Dutch inclined to reestablish good relations with Venezuela and did they have any suggestion about the procedure?
2. What was the purpose of sending a squadron to the West Indies?
3. Was it possible to solve the difficulties by ceding Curaçao to Venezuela, in exchange for money or territory on the continent?

The bluntness of the American inquiries was evident. Their directness contrasted dramatically with the obliqueness of the traditional European diplomacy in which Van der Does and his colleagues were schooled. No eye-witness account exists of the meetings of the Dutch Cabinet in which these questions were studied but one can imagine the raised eyebrows and nervous gestures of men not accustomed to frank confrontation. But Birney received his answers:

1. The government of the United States is not the first to offer mediation. We appreciate its friendly intensions, convinced as we are of its influence in Caracas. If the government of the United States would inform us of any Venezuelan proposals, we would be happy indeed, but further than that we cannot accept any interference.
2. The instructions of the squadron's commander are indeed far-reaching because they had to take into consideration many possibilities and the distance between the Netherlands and Curaçao hampers rapid communication. We cannot reveal the contents of those instructions but we do not hesitate to declare that in regard to foreign commerce and navigation all possible consideration will be observed and it is our wish that this squadron — sent also for training purposes — will have no other task.
3. The Dutch government assures most positively that there can be no question of ceding Curaçao.

The American Minister seemed satisfied and reported these replies to his government.[23] In turn, the Dutch Foreign Minister posed Birney a question: "If we use force against Venezuela in enforcing the opening of her ports, could that country count on material support from the United States?" "The United States," Birney assured Van der Does, "tries only to promote a peaceful solution." [24]

This answer sounded the death knell of Dalla Costa's peace initiative. It had caused nothing but confusion. Highly dissatisfied with his diplomat's performance, Guzmán Blanco sent him to Brazil, in those days a fate similar to deportation.

The incident clearly showed Venezuela's eagerness to resume normal relations with the Netherlands. This desire was also demonstrated by the visit of General Juan Francisco Pérez, a close friend of Guzmán Blanco's. In Curaçao he discussed with Brakel his government's genuine intention to arrive at a solution, but at the same time stated Guzmán Blanco's condition for peace: the replacement of Governor Wagner, considered the main obstacle to reconciliation. If that could be arranged, the president would be quite willing to compromise on all further disputes with the Netherlands. Brakel could only point out that Rojas had already requested Wagner's dismissal and that it was refused as an unacceptable interference in Dutch internal affairs.[25] Soon after this interview the Dutch chargé d'affaires left for Holland.

A curious incident added some strange color to the picture of broken relations. In Brussels, the former Dutch Foreign Minister and now envoy, Gericke van Herwijnen, was approached by the Venezuelan diplomat Pulido, who had played a role in the negotiations of 1871.[26] The latter startled the envoy, who had received him as an unofficial representative of Guzmán Blanco, with a sudden vitriolic outburst. Guzmán Blanco, he complained, had become a tyrant. The Venezuelan Congress, in flattering the president's limitless vanity and satisfying his insatiable hunger for money and power, was his willing accomplice. The situation had become unbearable. Preparations had been completed for a *coup,* for although Guzmán Blanco's term was nearing its end, through a combination of stimulated compliance with the law and adroit maneuvering, he was determined to stay in power.

For Curaçao, Pulido indicated, Guzmán Blanco would then become an even more obnoxious neighbor. The ports of Coro and Maracaibo would remain closed, while he would use the reclamations for indemnity as a pretext for any hostile action in what he would define as Venezuela's national interest. Curaçao's proximity heightened the possibility of troop disembarcation in as little as one night.

Because the closing of Coro and Maracaibo would lead to Curaçao's economic ruin, unemployment and discontent would grow, and the island would finally fall into the dictator's hands. "Do not be deceived," Pulido warned, "by the obliging attitude of the president, for it will last only until February 20." Once Guzmán Blanco's continued power was assured, the island's fate would be sealed. If he could take Curaçao by surprise, he would confidently expect the United States to settle the matter with The Hague, thus preventing the colony's return to the Dutch.

What could be done to obviate this situation? Undoubtedly it was in the Dutch interest to support any serious movement against the Illustrious American. This support could be arranged in such a way as not to compromise the Dutch government. Now Pulido came to the point:

What Guzmán Blanco's opponents needed was a large steamer able to carry many troops. It should be easy for the Dutch government to deliver such a ship through a commercial house at a foreign port. There the steamer would be transferred to Venezuelan patriots. Success was assured and prompt payment would follow.[27]

Gericke van Herwijnen was stunned by this undisguised attempt to involve The Hague in a Venezuelan *cuartelazo*. Immediately informed, the Dutch Foreign Minister for once behaved wisely by deciding to stay out of Venezuelan domestic trouble. Pulido's proposal was politely rejected.

Strangely enough, some Dutch coastal shipping seemed to have survived Guzmán Blanco's rigid regulations. On several occasions the Governor of Curaçao informed the home government that Venezuelan and Dutch schooners had arrived from Puerto Cabello with cargoes, and after unloading and reloading, departed again for Venezuela. Perhaps the fact that Generals Pulido (the brother of the former envoy) and Pulgar had left Trinidad for Europe caused the relaxation.[28] Thus a few Dutch ships were able to do business, although the unpredictable mood of the Venezuelan dictator made this hazardous.[29] The trade in war materiel, albeit sharply reduced in scope, was unfortunately a component of this shipping.[30] This is demonstrated by the *Julieta* affair. The captain of this schooner pretended his destination to be Puerto Rico, but the testimony of two members of his crew alerted Wagner to order an investigation.

La Voz Pública, a daily *guzmancista* paper circulating in the State of Carabobo, analyzed the seizure of the *Julieta*, property of the Jesurun House, and concluded that the ship was on "*una expedición baecista*".[31] The *Opinión Nacional* of Caracas commented somewhat bitterly: "If the planned expedition had been against Venezuela, instead of against Santo Domingo, would the Governor of Curaçao have shown the same zealous care in seizing the ship and investigating the cargo?"[32]

The Dutch Cabinet became concerned about this seizure, fearing an interpellation by Jesurun's aggressive lawyer Van Eck. But Wagner's position left no doubt. The *Julieta* had departed without a permit for war materiel; its captain had stated his intention to sail for Santo Domingo in support of a rebellion. Even Van Eck could not argue against these facts.[33]

More irritations followed. The bark *San Francisco* (owner unknown) of Aruba was seized by the Venezuelan coastal patrol. The skipper was fined 2,000 *venezolanos*, which were distributed among the commanders and crews of the two vessels responsible for the seizure. This measure was, of course, a powerful incentive to repeat the performance.[34]

In April, 1876, Stammann informed the Dutch Foreign Minister of the difficulties encountered by the Dutch schooner *Bella Petra,* seized in Puerto Cabello. But after a personal meeting between Stammann and Guzmán Blanco, the schooner was permitted to leave.[35] The clearest example of arbitrary behavior occurred with the Dutch schooner *Porteña* (owner David C. Henriques of Curaçao), seized in Barcelona. No reason for the seizure was given. The captain, however, happened to know Guzmán Blanco personally and traveled to Caracas to visit the president. In view of the circumstances, he was received amazingly well. Guzmán Blanco explained his diehard policy toward Curaçao, avowing at the same time that he had nothing personal against the captain. The latter was allowed to depart with his ship but the president told him: "Do not come back, or it will cost you 90 days." [36]

Though illustrating that some navigation between Venezuela and Curaçao continued, these examples show the risks which were incurred. The government, as Stammann pointed out, could legally order the detention of any vessel, national or foreign, for 20 to 100 days, on the mere suspicion of being engaged in clandestine traffic.[37] Although not openly opposing the transit of foreign steamers from Venezuelan ports to Curaçao and vice versa, the Venezuelan dictator applied all sorts of pressures to hinder this traffic.[38]

It was all part of a master plan, according to the German envoy. Not a single ship could leave the ports of La Guaira and Puerto Cabello, nor any other port of the Venezuelan littoral, for whatever destination without the president's permission. All these measures aimed at impeding the communication between Venezuelan ports and the Antilles, particularly Curaçao.[39]

Somewhat later that year Venezuelan policy to isolate Curaçao was confirmed by the Dutch envoy in Paris. Briefly, Van Zuylen van Nyevelt wrote that on February 20, 1877, Guzmán Blanco would transfer his power into the hands of Jacinto Gutiérrez, president of the High Federal Court, an incapable, old man, devoted to the Great Liberal. During the Gutiérrez interim, Guzmán Blanco would be the power behind the throne. One year later he could constitutionally present himself again as a candidate and his election would be only a matter of organization. Thus there would be no real interruption of his rule.[40]

This analysis of Venezuela's political future confirmed Pulido's predictions. Events occurred exactly as he had described. In spite of this, tensions between Venezuela and Curaçao relaxed considerably. The main reason undoubtedly was the departure of the Dutch squadron at the end of 1876. What had it accomplished? True, it had picked up the *Midas* at St. Thomas where the Venezuelan authorities had returned the schooner. But its presence in the Caribbean had been more harmful than helpful to good relations with the republic.

A little later the news arrived in the Netherlands that the president's tempestuous father had left for Paris. There were immediate speculations of an official mission to The Hague to negotiate a compromise.[41] The elder Guzmán's policy concerning Curaçao had not proved successful and perhaps he judged the time ripe to direct a new approach. He had openly confessed that he had never thought that the Dutch would risk a war for "that barren rock", which, far from bringing profit to the mother country, involved it in international difficulties and cost money. But the elder Guzmán was already 76 years old and had no official mission in mind. Nevertheless, his absence from Venezuela meant less tension. It was rumored that his son would soon follow.

Thinking of two aggressive leaders of Venezuelan foreign policy so close to The Hague, the Dutch Foreign Minister invited the former chargé d'affaires Brakel, now living in The Hague, to suggest provisions which would avoid future difficulties with Venezuela. "A complete prohibition," Brakel wrote, "of the export of war materiel will be the only solution and end the abuse which causes international problems." He suggested severe punitive measures.[42] But his ideas, good as they were, shared the fate of many other good ones. They were read, filed, and forgotten.

In discussions held at the end of the year on the colonial budget, the Second Chamber voiced much criticism of the Foreign Minister's policy, which, in its opinion, had incalculably damaged Curaçao's trade. The minister's demand that the two Venezuelan ports be opened before the claims of the republic would be investigated, argued the Chamber, had defeated its purpose.[43] What if the Venezuelan government had satisfied this demand? Then the Dutch government would have been forced to investigate the question of indemnity, which rested on the completely false premise that the colonial government of Curaçao had not fulfilled its duties as a neutral power. The Chamber concluded that the minister had failed to understand the problem. He should have declared as haughtily as had the Venezuelan envoy, that the matter could not be discussed.[44]

Thus the year 1876, which began with such poor expectations and ominous threats ended on this note. Even if the interrupted relations were no closer to restoration than before, the situation was much less explosive. Rapprochement between the colony and the republic was expected to be stimulated by the end of Guzmán Blanco's Septenio, and also by the expected resignation of Governor Wagner. However, by one of the strange quirks of fate the coming year would witness a totally different tactic of the Illustrious American to dominate "cruel Curaçao".

14. THE SALE OF CURAÇAO

The enlightened first King of the Netherlands, William I, dreamed of making Curaçao a West Indian Malta vital to the existence and prosperity of his kingdom, but the enormous expenditures involved soon brought second thoughts and the great plans evaporated into more modest ones.

The island's economy never really recovered from British occupation during most of the Napoleonic wars. The emancipation of the slaves in 1863 slowly strangled the languishing economy. Between 1867 and 1881, the Netherlands contributed over 2,200,000 guilders to cover administrative expenses of her islands in the Caribbean.[1] What remained of prosperity was solely that of a small number of merchants who depended largely upon trade with Venezuela. Many did not even speak Dutch, although they were strongly pro-Dutch by tradition.

In 1868 several members of the Second Chamber proposed abandoning Curaçao and dependencies because in that year alone the national treasury was drained of over 200,000 guilders for the island's administrative expenses.[2] The Minister for the Colonies rejected the idea primarily because it had not originated in the colony itself.

The proposal disturbed the Colonial *Raad* in Willemstad to no small degree. Abraham J. Jesurun, a member of this *Raad,* at once petitioned the governor to permit this body to demand from the Second Chamber an official statement against abandoning or selling the colony. In the *Raad* itself Jesurun proudly declared: "We are Dutch, of Dutch origin and education, and the inhabitants of this colony are attached to Holland." He implored the *Raad* to do its utmost to persuade the Dutch government to keep Curaçao.[3]

The *Raad* took immediate action. It appointed three of its members to draw up a report for the Second Chamber explaining why the island should continue under Dutch rule. This report was dispatched shortly afterwards.[4] It undoubtedly mirrored the outlook of the majority of the wealthy class.

But the interruption in official relations with Venezuela, combined with the heavy cost of sending two squadrons to the West, created a Dutch reaction against Curaçao. Thus it happened that during the debates on the King's Speech of 1876, a member of the Chamber proposed to cede that "dry rock" to Venezuela. Curaçao did not produce anything, and as long as the trade in war materiel was prohibited, it could not make any profit.[5]

This new proposal was not just someone's brainstorm, it was a serious motion. Other members of the Chamber protested that if enacted it would have the same consequences as the cession of the Dutch Guinea Coast to Great Britain a few years earlier. This had hurt the interests of both the Netherlands and the colonial inhabitants.[6] News of these proposals to abandon, cede, or sell Curaçao found their way to Caracas, and the Illustrious American quickly established his position as the most persistent promoter of the sale.

The first proposal to abandon Curaçao and the second to cede the island to Venezuela reflected concern for the high cost of maintaining indebted colonies. Both mirrored fear of the political implications of the war materiel trade and a desire for normal relations with Venezuela; both resulted from severe criticism of the present Dutch colonial policy. Van der Does found no broad support because he had difficulty in dealing with his critics. In answering the opposition he weakly maintained that it would not be fair for Curaçao to close its port, exclusively to please Venezuela, while the latter closed its own ports because of its bitterness against Curaçao, thus causing great damage to the island's trade. To give in to Venezuelan demands would be "contrary to the dignity of the Netherlands," he said.[7]

Despite pressure to the contrary, the port of Curaçao was restored to its "normal condition" for as long as Venezuela maintained her hostile attitude. None of the great powers, the Dutch Foreign Minister pointed out, had acted hastily in similar conflicts with the republic. Great Britain, for instance, had used her powerful navy cautiously when British ships were seized. His government, he observed, had applied the same temperance. Great restraint was needed to bring the Venezuelans to a *modus vivendi* safeguarding the interests of the island and the republic. Admittedly, Curaçao and Venezuela had to live together out of geographic necessity. A cession of the Curaçao islands, the minister concluded, definitely was not under consideration by his government.[8]

In the controversy concerning the cession or sale of the island, a curious incident caught everyone's attention for a moment. During the last week of September, 1876, Curaçao was hit by a severe hurricane.[9] The colonial government and private citizens immediately organized relief actions, but the most important aid came from Venezuela. The *Opinión Nacional* elaborated on the munificence of Guzmán Blanco, spreading a good deal of propaganda for the Great Liberal, and ended somewhat pompously: "Blessed be the man who protects the nations in their rights and supports humanity in its disasters." [10] Despite this bombast, Stammann was ordered to express The Hague's sentiments of appreciation, while Wagner followed suit. [11]

If this action raised hopes for a speedy rapprochement new suspicion and discontent soon dashed these. At the end of 1876 the Venezuelan government decreed sharper measures to curb coastal navigation: no ship could leave Venezuelan ports without a permit from the authorities. In Curaçao this measure was justly viewed as the worst blow to its weakened economy. [12] What little navigation had continued between the mainland coast and the Dutch Antilles came to a standstill. Ships of international lines now no longer dropped anchor in Willemstad, thus avoiding problems with Venezuelan port authorities. [13]

On February 8, 1877, Governor Wagner received an honorable discharge. It was not the result of outside pressure. There were some questions in the Second Chamber as to the honorable nature of Wagner's discharge and its implication of an official approval with respect to his line of conduct. [14] The Minister for the Colonies defended the governor. He had acted "in virtue of his instructions". Wagner's successor was Hendrik Kip, a former sea officer and a rather colorless figure completely lacking his predecessor's vigor.

In assessing Wagner as Governor in this most critical period of the colony's nineteenth century existence there remains some doubt about his performance. There is considerable evidence that his rigid and inflexible views markedly contributed to the Dutch Cabinet's rather shortrange analysis of the Venezuelan Question. He was a soldier and trained to obey, which he did. The orders he received from The Hague were, however, largely inspired by his own reports. Inexperienced and weak ministers for the Colonies and Foreign Affairs relied on his views, showed no initiative in developing their own thoughts on the matter, and displayed little understanding. Wagner understandably thought in terms of military power without regard for other avenues of solution. This was the basic mistake in his analysis of the conflict. He was honest, and courageous, hard working, and cool under fire. From hindsight it is evident that his term did not render lasting services to the colony.

When asked if the Netherlands docilely accepted the severe Venezuelan restrictions on navigation, the Dutch Foreign Minister told the Chamber that another power had approached the government to protest against the new measures. It had rejected this proposal because it was unwilling to take any step which could be interpreted as favoring the contraband trade. The difficulties with Venezuela, the Minister added, would have been settled long ago were it not for the press in both countries, which had become crucial in building up tensions.[15] In a memorandum written somewhat later the Foreign Minister repeated this accusation and blamed the press for creating a political hothouse. Rojas was described as being instrumental in influencing the press. He had, for instance, spent 15,000 guilders in Brussels for the publication of anti-Dutch articles and brochures.[16]

By now Curaçao's inhabitants seemed to have realized the disastrous course their economy was following, for the number of those protesting the trade in war materiel continuously increased. Some even planned to petition the King for an absolute prohibition, following Brakel's suggestion. This idea was abandoned when it was realized that such a petition would inform Guzmán Blanco of the supporters and opponents of trade restriction.[17] But the worsening economic depression resulting from the political impasse, worried especially the Curaçao merchant elite. They found an eloquent spokesman in a prominent Jewish lawyer, Abraham M. Chumaceiro, author of a dozen pamphlets on local issues. In his brochure *Is Curaçao te koop?* (Is Curaçao for Sale?) he insisted that this trade be stopped.[18]

In one of his last reports before his departure Wagner blamed the traumatic development on Guzmán Blanco's hostility towards Curaçao on his expulsion.[19] Wagner's successor Kip inherited this gross oversimplication of the Great Liberal's policy. Both governors believed their views confirmed by Venezuelan government contracts with Charles M. Neill, for an American steamship connection, and with Emile Wanner of Le Havre, the representative of a French company, which stipulated that the ships not drop anchor in Curaçao.[20] This myopic official view contrasted sharply with the awakening consciousness of the majority of the population.

Both governors may also have ridiculed Guzmán Blanco's suggestions to buy the island, but they did not understand one of his most important motives. Curaçao's contraband trade, he had said in his latest Congressional Message, was robbing the republic's treasury of almost 50 per cent of its income. This allegation, never proven but constantly repeated, did not exactly promote an atmosphere favorable to reconciliation. But Wagner as well as Kip saw the high Venezuelan import duties, averaging 40 per cent of the value of some commodities and sometimes reaching 75 per cent, as the most powerful stimulus to illicit trade.

Venezuela's licit imports for the fiscal year 1874/75, the last year that relations between the republic and Curaçao were normal, amounted to 17,300,000 *venezolanos* divided in the following manner:

From Germany	5,449,752	*venezolanos*
Spain	396,314	
Colombia	505,007	
United States	3,799,170	
France	2,598,033	
Great Britain	290,975	
Italy	48,618	
Danish colonies	19,512	
Spanish colonies	9,868	
French colonies	87,677	
British colonies	1,455,959	
Curaçao	2,642,960	

Curaçao's share in these imports was, as the figures show, around 16 per cent.[21] Wagner knew that British as well as French records showed twice the amount of exports to the republic as that which officially passed through Venezuelan customs.[22] Even if Curaçao's exports followed the same trend — which the former Curaçao governor denied — the 50 per cent figure seemed a wild exaggeration and had to be reduced to 16 per cent. But Wagner maintained that it was at the most 5 per cent, undoubtedly a much too low estimate, although the actual size of the smuggling has never been determined.

The Illustrious American, however, was not a man to be bothered with statistics. He felt the illicit trade as a thorn in his side and was willing to blame neither his inefficient administration and corrupt officials, nor the high duties levied as its causes. He only knew that it impeded the development of Venezuela's economy along the lines he had drawn.[23]

The idea of buying Curaçao must have come to him in the first weeks of 1877, before the end of the Septenio. He mentioned it publicly for the first time in his farewell address to Congress in February, 1877. He talked at great length about the island. "It does not produce anything," he said. "Its commerce could only sustain it-self through illegal means in competition with ours, because ours carries in addition the customs duties, and the expenses of some taxes." [24] In order to protect itself, the country had two choices: to continue the present situation and try to cut off all commercial ties with the island, or to buy it, even paying more than its actual value, and incorporate the island into Venezuela's national territory.[25]

Presenting these alternatives, Guzmán Blanco rejected a curious variant of U.S. suggestions as formulated by Birney. This was Rojas' overture at the beginning of June, 1875, to the Venezuelan Minister of Foreign Affairs Blanco. Rojas proposed to offer the Netherlands Venezuelan territory (supposedly Venezuelan Guiana) in exchange for Curaçao.[26] He was perhaps not aware that British Guiana was located between Dutch and Venezuelan Guiana.

Guzmán Blanco refused to trade mainland territory for the island as he preferred to buy it. In the hopes of facilitating a sale, the Illustrious American urged Rojas to use all his influence to get Brakel appointed as Governor of Curaçao.[27] He could work with Brakel, he said. In his speech to Congress he sketched a beautiful future: the purchase of Curaçao would immediately remove all present difficulties and prevent future ones, while it would be of vital importance to the republic's economy. It would not be easy, he warned, to convince the Dutch that this was really the only solution for stable relations between the Netherlands and Venezuela. And while Curaçao did not benefit the mother country, it would bring immeasurable profits to Venezuela.

> "The present Dutch Cabinet," the president continued, "seems to have dropped the unusual claim of the reopening of the ports of Coro and Maracaibo, seeking the *status quo* before the rupture of relations. However, I prefer the present situation, and believe that the Venezuelan government should maintain its inflexibility until the sale of Curaçao is accepted as the only solution satisfactory to both Holland and Venezuela, and imponderably advantageous to the island itself ... That day Curaçao will become our only port for imports, the great warehouse of merchandise and the center of our navigation ... After a quarter of a century Curaçao will become the richest and most beautiful city of the Caribbean." [28]

The speech revealed the president's awareness of Second Chamber proceedings. In that House, he said, the possibility of selling the island had already been discussed, but the Cabinet feared public reaction. If the Dutch government could overcome this wavering, the sale would set an example for Great Britain to follow with Trinidad.[29]

Soon after this speech Guzmán Blanco joined his family in Paris, leaving the government in the hands of his successor, Francisco Linares Alcántara. Alcántara, demonstrated his willingness to ease the continuing tensions by conferring the Certificate of the Bust of the Liberator on the new Governor of Curaçao.[30] The *Curaçaosche Courant* soon reported that navigation to Puerto Cabello and La Guaira had been freed of all restrictions, including the regulation of December 1876, which gave the executive the power to seize any ship in Venezuelan ports.[31] Optimism in Curaçao ran high, but for the time being these were all the concessions the new president made. The ports of Coro and Maracaibo remained closed.

In his message to Congress, the Great Democrat — as Alcántara was called — optimistically stated that "affairs with Holland" were being resolved and invited the legislature to discuss the problem of the closed ports. It became clear that the new Venezuelan government favored the reopening, and the president even hinted that the mediation of the United States could be the catalyst to bring Holland and Venezuela together.[32]

But this clear departure from the rigid lines devised by Guzmán Blanco did not meet with unanimous approval. This is well illustrated by a brochure published by General Joaquín Crespo under the title *Un Deber Cumplido* (A Duty Accomplished). In it Crespo repeated the old accusations: "Curaçao was the headquarters of all the enemies of Venezuelan peace ... it had no industry other than the traffic it had made in Venezuelan blood ... Curaçao has lived on our ruin and our calamities, speculating and enriching itself."

It was the old Guzmán Blanco refrain. The general could count on the former dictator's supporters, the Caracas merchants, who were even more willing to sacrifice their Coro and Maracaibo competitors than to ruin Curaçao. With this attitude prevailing among the capital's businessmen, the commercial house of Boulton committed itself to a most profitable program. It possessed two small steamers and controlled in the transfer of commodities between La Guaira, Puerto Cabello, and the closed ports. This monopoly had been granted by Guzmán Blanco, who was probably a silent partner.[33]

Consequently when Alcántara's move threatened the Boultons' profits the firm tried to bribe members of Congress to vote against the reopening of the closed ports, but to no avail. The Senate and somewhat later the House of Representatives voted to reopen them.[34] Thus an important obstacle to the improvement of relations between the Netherlands and Venezuela was removed.

The Governor of Curaçao immediately prohibited the export of war materiel under the Royal Degree of 1871.[35] Now everything seemed to point towards a quick resumption of the interrupted relations.

15. THE LONG INTERMEZZO

After six hectic years of turbulence in their relations, Venezuela and
Curaçao entered into an eighteen-year period of aloofness during which
the realities of the previous era appeared to have been a bad dream.
The lack of appreciable complaints, demands and trade gave these
years the appearance of a vacuum, whereas life before had possessed
the qualities of heat, noise, and ebullience. While the republic
experienced two other terms under the Great Liberal — the Quinquenio
(1879-84) and the Aclamación (1886-88) — the island went through
the convulsions of a slowly strangling economy.

After delivering his farewell address, Guzmán Blanco left Venezuela
in 1877 to serve his country in various European nations as Minister
Plenipotentiary. Shortly afterward the republic entered a new revolutionary period. The new rebellion, organized and financed in Trinidad,
was headed by General Ignacio Pulido, a former refugee in Curaçao
and brother of the diplomat Lucio Pulido.[1]

From its inception the *pulidista* revolt encountered nothing but set-
backs. It died in its own cradle, the State of Bolívar, and its leader was
taken prisoner. The country's problems increased with Alcántara's sudden
death in November, 1878. The old *guzmancista*, General Jacinto Gutiérrez, succeeded the Great Democrat. Several factors then combined to
stimulate violent anti-*guzmancista* sentiment among the populace, culminating in the destruction of statues erected by the Illustrious American
in his own honor. It soon became apparent that the Gutiérrez regime
was unable to inspire national cohesion. A new revolt called for the
reinstallation of Guzmán Blanco, the weak government collapsed and
Guzmán Blanco cabled his decision to accept the presidency.

The Illustrious American had spent almost two years in Paris, and
they had not been very successful ones. One of the reasons for his
appointment as Minister Plenipotentiary was the dictator's fundamental
desire to purchase Curaçao. He had discussed this project with the
French Foreign Minister Waddington, who, aware of the Illustrious
American's high position and the probability that he would again
become president of Venezuela, had listened politely. Waddington then
informed the Dutch Minister Resident of this meeting.[2]

The absence of records to substantiate Guzmán Blanco's claims that he sincerely labored in this project makes it difficult to evaluate his assertions. The sale or cession of Curaçao was in the air those days, and various schemes abounded. Most persistent was the story of a cession or sale to the German Empire. In September, 1878 the Dutch envoy in Berlin informed the new Foreign Minister in The Hague, W. van Heeckeren van Kell, of persuasive news items in the German press elaborating on plans to acquire the island of Curaçao as a naval base for the German fleet.[3] Although Germany was beginning to consolidate her position as a great power, her press did not unanimously express enthusiasm for such an acquistion. Wrote the *Nationale Zeitung*: "Imagine Curaçao a German island and the German Reich at war with a naval power. In such a case we would need our men-of-war to protect our own coasts and thus would be unable to send a fleet out for the protection of Curaçao." [4] The argument was convincing, together with another that the provisioning of more than 20,000 people in time of war would be impossible "particularly if one realizes that pea sausages and similar items are not very proper for the tropics." [5]

Another rumor had it that The Hague was willing to hand Curaçao over to the Germans in exchange for Embden. Late in 1879, the Dutch envoy in Washington, Von Pestel, informed The Hague that in a recent meeting with U.S. Secretary of State William M. Evarts the possibility of the cession or sale of Curaçao was discussed in reference to reports in various American papers.[6] Similar information reached The Hague from Brussels, where a former American diplomat, Henry Shelton Sanford, discussed the topic with the Dutch envoy there.

Situated between "Greedy England and Grasping Germany" [7] the Dutch were reluctant to make closer contact with the nation whose rapidly expanding trade relations in the Caribbean were watched with apprehension — the United States. That Uncle Sam was already a dangerous political and economic competitor of Great Britain and Germany did not seem to awaken the new Dutch Foreign Minister to the necessity for a new approach. Leaders in the United States were certainly far from indifferent to the danger of a German possession so close to their shores. Their interest in a possible change of master of the island was understandable. The Dutch saw this interest as another threat to their control over the island and resented it.

What Guzmán Blanco did in Paris to realize his plans for a purchase of the island is far from clear. It seems probable that he had planned to visit The Hague to discuss the issue. But in his two years' residence in the French capital he apparently did not find an opportunity to go. The furthest he went was to the Dutch embassy.[8] The Hague, eager to avoid all semblance of personal enmity or public irritation, was willing to receive him as long as a discussions would not acquire an official character. Within this pattern of thought an eventual cession of Curaçao, the Dutch Foreign Minister said, could never be placed on the agenda.[9]

Whatever his final intentions, the increasing confusion in Venezuela prevented Guzmán Blanco from going to The Hague. Before he returned to Caracas, he met the Dutch envoy and outlined his plans for the purchase of the island. With this in mind he would probably be forced, he admitted, to undo many measures of the Alcántara government. He specifically mentioned the two ports closed under his first administration. If the Dutch government was not willing to reach an understanding, he would again have to close those ports, not as a hostile act, he hastened to add, but as a political and economic necessity.[10]

Two points were clear from the beginning: The fact that two Dutch naval demonstrations had not accomplished anything bolstered Venezuelan morale and confidence. However, it had weakened the Dutch through loss of prestige and heavy expenses. Thus on the assumption that he could negotiate from strength, Guzmán Blanco evaluated the continuing possession of Curaçao as a burden on the Dutch taxpayer, the more so because "the present state of defense of the island was miserable".[11] Both points disguised the subtle threat of a possible attack.

Only an ignoramus could be unaware of the fact that his words foreshadowed troubles. These worries were little relieved by Guzmán Blanco's short visit to Willemstad on his way back home. The meeting with Kip was correct but cool. He then tried to convince Venezuelan refugees on the island that they had nothing to fear from him and could safely return home.[12] Few, if any, trusted him. He also called on some Curaçao merchants notorious for their trade in war materiel. What he discussed with them is not known.

As soon as he arrived in Caracas, the Illustrious American initiated a political reform which took priority even over his Curaçao project.[13] He drafted a new constitution which gave the executive greater power and strengthened his grasp on public life.[14] A new reorganization of the "diplomatic debts" was the second item on his agenda. He urged his puppet Congress to issue debentures at 4 per cent interest in order to replace the "diplomatic debts". None of the foreign countries involved was happy; all anticipated only more confusion from this change.

The proposals, once accepted by Congress, would end monthly payments to the legations and eliminate the small possibility of using political pressure on the Caracas elite. Pretending that the country was losing money under the old arrangement, he urged Congress to accept the unilateral changes after a deadline was set for foreign governments to respond.[15]

He then turned to the realization of his threats. Only such ports as La Guaira, Puerto Cabello, and Ciudad Bolívar, which he completely controlled and which Alcántara had opened to international traffic, were deliberately left open because of needed new war materiel.[16] Governor Kip of Curaçao showed considerable political understanding and self-discipline by continuing, with the approval of The Hague, any such exports. But Guzmán Blanco made it clear upon assuming power and initiating the Quinquenio, that other ports such as Coro and Maracaibo would remain closed. At the same time he openly proclaimed a most sincere desire for Holland's friendship. Aware of his rising unpopularity among the inhabitants of the western coastal regions, he was slow to carry out his threats.[17]

The cautious attitude of the Dutch reflected their fear of increasing conflict with the republic and its unpredictable leader. Indeed, new problems soon appeared. In May, 1879, Governor Kip received a letter from Eduardo Calcaño, then Venezuelan Foreign Minister, warning him that "the enemies of Venezuela" had again found refuge on the island and were conspiring against the republic. Kip was requested to take "the repressive measures expected of a good neighbor".[18] Soon an extension of this demand followed asking for the expulsion of General Alejandro S. Ybarra, who had left his country for the island for private rather than political reasons.[19] Backed by The Hague, Kip denied the request.

The Venezuelan press promised no relaxation of tensions. An article in the *Opinión Nacional* stressed the point that the Illustrious American had taken the initial step towards a reconciliation with the Netherlands by visiting the Dutch envoy in Paris. Now The Hague had to prove its sincerity if it wanted a return to normal relations. The Hague, it complained, did nothing.[20]

Sometimes old colonial regulations provoked irritations which could have been avoided by better legislation. An outdated law from 1822 required foreign ships to store cargoes of war materiel in the government's warehouse as soon as they dropped anchor in Curaçao. But the safeguards of the Royal Decree of 1871, prohibiting the exportation of war materiel, impeded the reloading of these cargoes when the ships were ready to leave. In 1822 the possibility of such a prohibition was completely overlooked. Uninformed captains regularly complained about this procedure, and their complaints had the support of their governments.[21] Irritating as they were, these shortcomings of Dutch colonial legislation never reached the danger point, as captains could usually produce enough official evidence that the war materiel their ships carried originated in their country and was registered there.[22]

Venezuela's cargoes were treated in a similar fashion. In September, 1879 General Nicolás M. Gil, Minister of the Interior of the Quinquenio regime, visited Willemstad and asked the governor's permission to take some Venezuelan war materiel, stored in the government's warehouse, back to his country. The governor, under strict orders of The Hague not to permit exceptions, refused because the export would not satisfy the 1871 degree. This refusal apparently did not spoil Gil's mood. He assured Kip that his government thus far was favorably impressed with the attitude of the colonial authorities and urged him not to believe rumors about the closing of the ports of Coro and Maracaibo.[23] Some concern remained, Gil admitted. Persuasively he explained the Great Liberal's irritation with the island's press, especially *El Imparcial*. Kip, taken by surprise, promised to investigate the matter and the two parted good friends.[24] High hopes of a speedy reconciliation were raised.

In the fall of 1879, these expectations collapsed amidst rising fears of a Venezuelan *coup de main* to occupy the island. Gil had informed Guzmán Blanco, rightly or wrongly, that the people who had overthrown his statues during the interval between the Septenio and Quinquenio all resided in Curaçao.[25] The Great Liberal, irritated by the frustration of his Curaçao project and aggravated by several minor irritants (among them the slowness of the Dutch government to grant the *exequatur* to Hugo Sassen, Venezuelan consul in Amsterdam) permitted a more aggressive tone in the Venezuelan press.[26] The Dutch government reacted unwisely. Despite two previous costly failures the suggestion to send a squadron to the Caribbean almost prevailed. The unsuccessful experiences of earlier years had left, however, some trace of common sense and a few weak protests questioned its effectiveness. Plans to send a training squadron to the Cape Verde islands had already been conceived. Now a West Indian prolongation was added in case of an emergency. If necessary the commander could sail immediately from there to Curaçao, arriving within two weeks.[27] Under these circumstances the Venezuelan government could hardly accuse the Dutch of aggressiveness, The Hague assumed.[28] It was not yet a candid admission of former errors, but it was a small step toward understanding the Venezuelan Question. The King's Speech ignored relations with the republic but expressed hopes for Curaçao's future, not so much because of a slightly encouraging revival of trade but because of the discovery of phosphate nitrates in the colony and their possible exploitation.[29]

At the end of January, 1880 a new rebellion shook Venezuela. Starting in Ciudad Bolívar it spread rapidly over the eastern states. Caracas immediately proclaimed a blockade of the Orinoco delta.[30] No sooner had this news reached Curaçao than General Colina, again a refugee on the island and the rumored head of the revolt, departed to join his colleague, General José Pío Revollo, the initiator of this new crisis. But the blockading vessels of the Venezuelan government prevented Colina from disembarking. A similar mishap occurred to Level de Goda and other anti-*guzmancistas* who were trying to return to the fatherland from Trinidad.[31] The uprising lacked popular support and was soon crushed, but Guzmán Blanco, intensely angered by these continuous interruptions of his rule found good reason to retaliate by making serious threats against Curaçao as well as Trinidad.

The dictator's mood is perfectly caught in an aggressive article in the *Opinión Nacional*:

"We must again direct the attention of our government to what is going on in Curaçao.[32] Against all rules of international law, the authorities of this island not only permit conspiracies to be plotted in its territory, a behavior as scandalous as that of those who overthrew the statues, but they also place the island's press at the disposal of those fugitives . . ."

Even more vitriolic was a strident call for revenge in Guzmán Blanco's message to Congress. Both Curaçao and Trinidad were blamed for sheltering the enemies of his regime, showing a devilish callousness by granting refuge to the stubborn enemies of the peace of Venezuela.[33]

Guzmán Blanco suggested two solutions. One was to close the ports of Coro, Ciudad Bolívar, and Maracaibo and move the customs offices to Puerto Cabello and Carúpano to prevent the loss of desperately-needed government revenues. But the Great Liberal thought another course of action more advisable: subject imports from the Antilles to differential duties. This policy would kill two birds with one stone.

It would deliver a crushing blow to the languishing economies of both Trinidad and Curaçao and, at the same time, would promote direct commercial intercourse with Europe and the United States. If these islands continued to sabotage the republic's economy by their refusal to curb the contraband trade and to introduce measures desired by the country's government, this second solution was the only choice. Although he did not say it in so many words, the measures mentioned doubtlessly meant the prohibition of war materiel exports and the stricter supervision of Venezuelan refugees.[34]

As Corporaal rightly observes, this combination of "additional duties" and threats to fulfill his demands gave Guzmán Blanco's policy in essence the character of a countervailing action aimed directly against the Antilles, particularly Curaçao.[35] Only a narrow view, insensitive to the complexities of the question, however, would attribute to the Illustrious American the sole motivations of vengeance and retaliation. His desire to expand Venezuela's economic bases might have been closer to his heart, although increasing his and his friends' fortunes was a strong bait. The main reason for his differential duties must, therefore, be sought in his commitment to the political and economic plan which emerged in the Quinquenio to establish direct commercial ties with Europe and the United States — in other words to eliminate the Antilles as middleman. The intermediate trade of Curaçao with Coro and Maracaibo and of Trinidad with the Orinoco region had to be eliminated for the good of Venezuela's trade and treasury and for himself and such friends as the Boultons and the Röhls. The concept of differential duties did not originate with him. More than fifty years earlier Bolívar had tried to introduce additional duties on all commodities not directly originating in Europe or the United States.[36] With the vehement protests of foreign countries the question was dropped, but the precedent had been established.

In the intervening fifty years the situation had changed drastically. Gran Colombia had distintegrated into three states, and the small needs of long ago had increased considerably. What had not changed was the depressing fact that Venezuela was still almost completely dependent on foreign imports. The country had not industrialized, and the expanding population only multiplied the need for such imports.

Guzmán Blanco was fully aware of this intolerable situation, which deeply hurt his national pride. That Venezuelan shopkeepers, bypassing the direct contact with European and American commercial firms, bought commodities in Curaçao was hard for him to swallow. His patriotic feelings were undoubtedly mixed with those of self-interest. He was a silent partner in some business firms, and his views also hinged on the advantages their increasing profits would offer him if the middle-man, i.e. Curaçao, could be eliminated. Differential duties would strongly stimulate direct trade, strengthen the position of the wholesale merchants, especiallly in Caracas, and would probably encourage the building of a Venezuelan merchant marine. Small businessmen, how-ever, feared that these duties would hasten their decline by bolstering big business.

It is apparent that Guzmán Blanco had been thinking within this framework for some time. To assess his intentions correctly one must recognize the various motives which moved him to a decision. Were the duties his means of diverting national attention away from domestic problems? Were they only meant to convince the Netherlands and Great Britain that they would be wiser and would save their taxpayers' money by selling Curaçao and Trinidad? Were they meant to be a haggling tool in the negotiations of a commercial treaty with those countries and to wrest an agreement on war materiel exports from them? Were they intended to pressure the expulsion of certain refugees? If, as he claimed, he intended to promote Venezuelan interests without regard for his private gain, why did he not introduce a more efficient system of duties which in the long run would have fomented direct trade without immediate ruinous consequences for the Antilles? [37]

Also difficult to assess is Rojas' new approach to the Venezuelan Question. He had resided in Paris for some time when he suddenly reopened talks on the renewal of diplomatic relations between the republic and the Netherlands. Venezuela's political and economic situation, he informed the Dutch envoy in London, had improved considerably. Guzmán Blanco was well aware of the measures taken by the colonial authorities to stop the contraband trade, and Rojas himself was familiar with the Dutch position that Venezuela should drop her claims. Because the rupture had originally taken place while he was representing his country, he was pleased to act as the inter-mediary in negotiating a restoration of relations and to travel to The Hague to ensure success.[38] The ploy, supposedly initiated to sound out Dutch feelings on normalization, failed to work.

In the summer of 1880 the deadline for governments to respond to the Venezuelan proposal on a reorganization of the debt payments expired. The new measure caused deep concern among foreign govern-ments. Lord Salisbury roundly rejected it "on the grounds that it might involve responsibilities which would not be in accordance with the interests of this country." [39] Strangely enough, some claimants would receive more than before: the monthly amount of 2,428 *venezolanos* formerly credited to the Dutch would increase to 3,667 because the Venezuelan government was willing to recognize some claims not previously included in this category.[40] But the fact that payments would be in bonds issued at 3 per cent interest caused extreme discontent. Some foreign governments protested, fearing they would receive valueless paper, but to no avail.[41]

The negative attitude manifested by most foreign powers moved Caracas to a small effort at accommodation. The regime revised the diplomatic debts so that the total amounts would be newly established and paid off monthly to the respective legations in paper issued by the government.[42] The new payments as compared with the former ones were as follows:

	Debts in *venezolanos*	Payments before May 1879 in *venezolanos*	Promised payments after May 1879 in *venezolanos*
France	798,255,67	1,684	2,760,50
United States	1,461,790,83	6,140	5,006,19
Gr. Britain	448,208,81	886	1,550,06
Denmark	40,310,29	47	144,08
Netherlands	1,047,726,64	2,428	3,667
Spain	1,926,114,41	8,548	6,700,20

Efforts toward unanimous protest failed, and France soon recalled her envoy. Venezuela retaliated by recalling Rojas.[43]

A further retaliation against the Dutch refusal to reopen negotiations occurred in February, 1881, when Venezuela suddenly stopped payments which until then had been made on a fairly regular basis, despite the interruption of diplomatic relations.[44] The old strategy of official blackmail was reapplied to force The Hague to comply with certain demands in the case of the *Riqueza*. This schooner (owner unknown) left Curaçao on August 18, 1880 destined for Bonaire. It carried eight Venezuelan refugees who had slipped aboard with rifles and gunpowder and forced the captain to put them ashore on the Venezuelan coast.

Animosity flared up again with the interception of correspondence between known anti-*guzmancistas* in Curaçao and Venezuela revealing a new conspiracy. Guzmán Blanco tried another approach in sending a special representative, General Felix E. Bigotte, to Willemstad. Bigotte handed the governor around 50 of these letters and the usual demand for expulsion.[45] After an investigation by the Attorney General clearly proved the complicity of some refugees, the governor complied with the demand and fourteen Venezuelans were forced to leave the island.[46] Caracas' complaints about anti-*guzmancista* publications in Curaçao were not redressed due to lack of sufficient proof.

Unsatisfied with the attitude of the Curaçao authorities, the *Opinión Nacional* loudly proclaimed its strong anti-Dutch feelings, underscoring the "peculiar neutrality" of the island and "its eternal threat to the peace and the prosperity of the republic".[47] The Hague was not impressed by these outbursts, they had occurred too often. The King's Speech of 1881 did not mention Venezuela at all, nor did Guzmán Blanco refer to the Dutch Question in his message to Congress that year.

But his next message was less benevolent. Tapping as many sources as he could muster he strongly outlined the intolerable situation:

"International relations are well maintained, except with Holland and Colombia, which continue to be interrupted. The former, because Holland is not willing to investigate the just reclamations of Venezuela with regard to the participation of some inhabitants of the island of Curaçao in the revolution of 1874 . . ." [48]

A bad omen for the future was the following paragraph: "Another measure which would contribute to achieving our goal is that of the introduction of differential duties". The president was making up his mind after two years of vacillation. He decided on an additional duty of 30 per cent on all foreign merchandise imported via the Antilles.

Thus his long-planned strategy finally took form in this "differential duties" project. Maybe the unwillingness of the Governor of Curaçao to muzzle the press removed the last restraint he might have felt. Although not completely indifferent to good international relations, Guzmán Blanco was often ruthless with regard to others' views. Neither the recall of the French chargé d'affaires nor the possibility of a French-Dutch alignment against him disturbed the Illustrious American.[49] His fine political instincts warned him that neither France nor the Netherlands would resort to arms as long as Great Britain refused to join them. And the latter was not ready. Her South African ambitions and Guiana problems diverted her attention.[50] This lack of unity among the European powers gave Guzmán Blanco a strong political hand and he played it extremely well.

His masterly cunning is revealed in an article in the *Opinión Nacional*, (written by a columnist paid by the president, as Governor Kip suggested) [51] which refers to Venezuela's problems with various foreign powers. It commented rather optimistically and self-assuredly: "England finds herself in a bind similar to France, but has not acted the same way [recalling her ambassador]. Lord Granville has declared he will not resort to these extreme measures [i.e. the use of force]." [52] Only Holland, "seems to be inclined to make common cause with France and has declared herself ready to put a naval force at the disposal of the French republic to exercise pressure on Venezuela." [53] The source of this information was not disclosed. This type of propaganda probably stifled internal opposition against the Great Liberal and promoted national feelings. Guzmán Blanco knew this quite well and profited from it.

In May of that same year 1811, Congress rubber-stamped the presidential proposals for an additional duty of 30 per cent levied on:

1. all produce, merchandise, and livestock proceeding from foreign colonies and imported through the ports of entry of the Republic as well as those proceeding from the ports of Europe or the United States of North America, destined for Venezuela, and transshipped in said colonies into other vessels, which are to bring them to the country;

2. all produce, merchandise, and livestock shipped in Europe or the United States of North America destined for the eastern or western ports of the Republic, to which vessels having them aboard do not propose to proceed, may be transshipped in Carúpano, La Guaira, or Puerto Cabello in order to continue their voyage to said ports, and may also be examined and cleared in any of these free ports of transshipment in order afterwards to be forwarded to their destination in coasting vessels.

   In this last case there shall be allowed on the duties on merchandise, produce, and livestock, thus imported, such a rebate as the National Executive may fix as compensation for the extra expenses incurred on them . . . [54]

Besides demonstrating Guzmán Blanco's economic strategy, this law violated existing commercial treaties. The dictator's indifference to these violations was not shared by others, particularly Great Britain and the United States. [55] The differences with the former country over the Guiana border question made the British protests rather pointless.

The United States fared better. Although, already, her economic expansion had assumed imperialistic tendencies, she still had no colonies. Her steamship company, the *Red D Line,* however, was threatened by the new laws. Repeated protests of the American minister in Caracas caused the Guzmán Blanco regime to reconsider some details of the new regulations in order to gain an ally against Great Britain in the pending border dispute. An additional amendment in January, 1883, resulted from these reconsiderations. The Venezuelan government thus acceded to the wishes of the United States.[56] This agreement was also beneficial to Curaçao by freeing the island from some of the damaging consequences of the original concept.[57]

The differential duties dramatically affected the island's economy in spite of the small relief provided by the law in 1883. Trade dropped alarmingly. Whereas Curaçao's imports totaled 5,559,412 guilders in 1880, these slumped to 3,506,620 guilders in 1882, and to 3,123,221 guilders in 1883. This steady decrease caused an exodus of Curaçao merchants. For instance, the Jewish population numbering around 1,000 in 1865, had dwindled to 750 by 1886.[58]

Curaçao narrowly missed a second blow when Colombia followed Venezuela's example and levied a similar tax beginning in May, 1887. In the six years between 1881 and 1887, Curaçao's merchants had greatly extended their trade with this country to compensate for the barriers raised by Venezuela. Many Curaçao firms had even established branches in Barranquilla and other coastal towns. The imposition of this new law would have killed this budding commerce. Thanks to the intervention of a Dutch Jewish consul, David Lopes Cohen, the Colombian government abolished the tax.[59]

In the midst of the anxieties caused by the introduction of these additional duties a curious event occurred. Pedro Luis Brion, former admiral of Gran Colombia and a native of Curaçao, had been buried in 1821 on the grounds of the Rozentak plantation on the island. His grave had never attracted Venezuelan attention until 1877 when Ramón Azpurua, the author of several hundred short biographies of *hombres notables* (famous men) of the War of Independence visited Curaçao and published a short sketch on Brion's life.[60]

Azpurua's account and the forthcoming 1883 Bolívar centennial aroused Guzmán Blanco's interest. He astutely calculated the gains his public image could derive from manipulating this celebration to his personal advantage. In August, 1881, he decreed that the mortal remains of the "illustrious precursor Admiral Luis Brion" be interred in the newly created National Pantheon in Caracas. Despite the interruption in official relations, negotiations with colonial authorities proceeded smoothly.[61] Brion's body was exhumed and in April 1882, together with that of General Daniel Florencio O'Leary, entombed in the burial place of Venezuela's heroes. In Curaçao there was much praise for Guzmán Blanco's initiative.[62] However, his subsequent request for Dutch representation to the 1883 Bolívar celebrations caused a problem of protocol because of the interrupted relations. The Dutch Cabinet finally decided to leave the matter to the Governor of Curaçao. Instead of the Netherlands, her troublesome colony was represented in Caracas. Somehow everyone overlooked this irony.

Despite the favorable impression made by Curaçao's spontaneous and enthusiastic collaboration in the Brion festivities, relations with the republic did not improve. While the *guzmancista* Foreign Minister congratulated a new Governor of Curaçao for his cooperation, the latter received new complaints about the Curaçao press and its publications which "preached murder" against Venezuela.[63] As usual the complaints were soon followed by demands for expulsion, in this case that of General Eleazar Urdaneta, the recognized leader of a new revolt in the making, together with some other exiles.[64]

The new governor, admonished by his superior in The Hague, complied with the demand. An investigation proved the refugees' complicity in subversive activities and they were expelled.[65] This softened Guzmán Blanco sufficiently to decorate the governor. In presenting the medal Boye, the commercial agent of Venezuela, optimistically and erroneously assured him that the question of the additional duties would soon be filed in some dusty closet.[66]

But a little later in the year the president's message to Congress erased any hopes the Antillians might have had regarding these duties. It had not been possible, Guzmán Blanco said adamantly, to restore normal relations with the Netherlands because her government stubbornly refused to discuss the rightful reclamations of the republic.[67] Thus the year 1882 proceeded with no change in the international situation, and the gloomy mood of the Curaçao merchants worsened as they saw their trade decline. The colonial government was powerless, caught in a political trap. The decisions were made in The Hague and the matter received scant attention there. "The situation in the West Indies," the Cabinet had the King say in his Speech of that year, "is not unsatisfactory." [68]

At the end of 1882 the Antillean gloom was alleviated by news of a meeting between the Dutch and Venezuelan ministers in Washington.

Simón Camacho, the Venezuelan envoy, told his Dutch colleague Von Pestel how deeply he was concerned about the Dutch Venezuelan Question. He thought the moment opportune to end it. In his country, he said, all was quiet with Guzmán Blanco in absolute control; conditions permitted the return of some of his most outspoken opponents. Camacho called Von Pestel's attention to the open invitation contained in the President's Congressional message of 1882 to discuss the problems under the mediation of the United States.[69] The Dutch, as adamant as the Illustrious American before, refused such mediation. U.S. willingness to assume this role is questionable; she had her own specific problems with Guzmán Blanco around this time.[70]

However, as a result of these conversations, it finally dawned on The Hague that the existing situation was untenable and should be remedied. Again the Venezuelan Question was discussed in several Cabinet meetings. A new Governor of Curaçao, Nicolaas van den Brandhof, out of ignorance or shortsightedness, proposed the repeal of the prohibition of war materiel exports as a means of pressuring Venezuela to give up the high surtax. The Cabinet, wisely, rejected this proposal.[71]

Again nothing happened. The King's Speech of 1883 made only scant reference to the West Indian affairs: "Our attention is directed to the consequences expected for the Curaçao colony from the digging of the Canal of Panama." [72]

Guzmán Blanco's Congress was hardly better informed than the Dutch Second Chamber. In a December, 1883 message, the Illustrious American mentioned with satisfaction "the diplomatic and naval representation of this colonial government at the centennial celebration of the Illustrious Bolívar." Congress intoxicated by these words, authorized the president to propose the reopening of negotiations on the restoration of relations.[73]

As usual, the high expectations were of short duration. Now it was Curaçao that blundered into irritating reactions because of a series of articles in El Imparcial which were not silenced by the government. Fervent hopes for a change of rule in Venezuela were not realized either. Guzmán Blanco's grasp on power was strong enough to permit him again to leave the country. Before he left in 1884, he stated in his farewell address that Venezuela had good relations "with all friendly nations".[74]

The Bolívar celebrations had one favorable result: they restored written contact between The Hague and Caracas. It consisted mainly of an exchange of courteous platitudes. In January, 1885 a Dutch war frigate, the *Tromp,* visited several Venezuelan ports and was well received. That same year saw a new rebellion under Generals Pulgar and Urdaneta in alliance with José M. Rojas. The former representative had defected from Guzmán Blanco and became his bitter enemy.[75] The rebellion lasted only a few weeks; General Crespo's position as acting president was never seriously threatened. It pleased him that the colonial authorities had denied port entry to the rebel ship *Justicia,* labelled a pirate by Caracas. Boye defined the policy of Curaçao as "well-understood neutrality". The *Justicia,* with some frustrated rebel leaders aboard, then sailed to Santo Domingo. Official Venezuelan complaints were subsequently directed against this country.[76]

In 1886, Guzmán Blanco assumed the presidency for the third and last time, initiating a period known in Venezuelan history as the Aclamación (1886-88). During these two years the relationship with Curaçao underwent no change. The Dutch Foreign Minister in describing this standstill to the Dutch envoy in Paris wrote: "The restoration of normal diplomatic relations to which His Majesty's government certainly is not disinclined, because there is no animosity between our two nations, has to be initiated by Venezuela." [77] This cautious diplomatic wording meant in everyday language that the Dutch were eager to resume a normal relationship.

Although efforts at improvement failed, partly because of the overly formal attitude of the Dutch, the scarce correspondence between Caracas and The Hague of those years now included Willemstad. The new Governor of Curaçao, Van den Brandhof, after his initial error in analyzing the situation, showed more initiative and insight than his immediate predecessors.[78] In spite of a drastic decline in government revenues caused by severe losses in trade, he provided the island with a pontoon bridge connecting the two parts of Willemstad separated by the St. Ann Bay, previously linked by a ferry.[79] In 1889, Curaçao was included in a cable connection between Venezuela, Haiti, and Cuba.

Van den Brandhof also attempted, under The Hague's supervision, to mend diplomatic relations with the republic. There seemed some hope for improvement when it was learned that Guzmán Blanco might visit Curaçao on his return from France in 1886. Discerning a favorable opportunity to take the initiative and envisioning an end to the impasse in relations, The Hague agreed to authorize the Curaçao governor to act as a "go-between". He was cautioned, however, not to set his expectations too high. The Dutch Cabinet expressed a realistic doubt concerning a compromise with respect to the additional duties.

Guzmán Blanco did not disembark in Curaçao and consequently Van den Brandhof did not have an opportunity to advance his views. The latter asked the Dutch consul in Caracas, Nicolaas F. Hellmund, to deliver his message of congratulation to the Venezuelan president upon the assumption of his third term and if possible, to see what could be done about the duties.[80] Hellmund spent a cordial half hour with the Venezuelan dictator. Out of the blue sky the latter observed that the restoration of normal relations with The Hague was going well and that during his stay in Europe he had strongly promoted a speedy conclusion.[81] What still had to be done would not cause any problem, and he added "I believe that through the mediation of Mr. Van den Brandhof a definite arrangement can be reached." [82] During this time there is no documentary evidence of a concrete approach by Guzmán Blanco except his own word. The delicate topic of additonal duty was not touched.[83]

Again, any optimism sparked by these words evaporated with the realization that the president's imagination had run away with him. He had not been to The Hague, nor is there proof of any contact in this period with the Dutch envoy in Paris. Supported by metropolitan businessmen, Guzmán Blanco assumed power and revived the policy of his earlier administrations. In April, 1887 a rather roughly worded request was handed to the Governor of Curaçao for the expulsion of three prominent Venezuelan officers in exile on the island: Pedro Obregón Silva, Luis Level de Goda, and Luis María Diaz. Díaz had caused earlier friction and wisely declined Guzmán Blanco's offer of amnesty made in 1882, continuing his directorship of the Colegio Vargas in Curaçao.[84] Level de Goda, the author of a political and military history of Venezuela, was also well known on the island. Again on a collision course with the Guzmán Blanco regime, he judged it wiser to remain in his former refuge. Silva, a former military man, had exchanged the sword for the pen and as the editor of La Nación fervently expounded what the Illustrious American defined as a "reactionary attitude".[85] Obviously his commitment had caused the displeasure of the Great Liberal. Their expulsion was requested in sharp terms and, as usual, was followed by some unveiled threats, in this case the closing of the few Venezuelan ports where some trifling traffic with Curaçao was condoned.[86]

Although far from happy about the note's insulting wording, Van den Brandhof hesitated over the course he should follow. He did not disregard his Attorney General's advice not to heed the demand, but playing for time he ordered an investigation.[87] This had the advantage of cooling heated emotions. It was disclosed that the accused exiles had contributed to some publications which could be considered insulting to Guzmán Blanco, especially those written by a fourth man soon to be added to the list: Jacob Moreno, director of the weekly review *El Observador*.[88]

In his courteous reply to Caracas' demands Van den Brandhof pointed out that under colonial law there was freedom of the press and that an offense to the leader of another nation should not be considered an incitement to revolution or conspiracy against peace. At worst these publications constituted grounds for the Venezuelan president to file complaints against their authors in order to initiate criminal action.[89] His answer was well-worded and refrained from any reference to the Venezuelan threat to Curaçao's commerce.

Far from pacifying Caracas, this response increased its irritation and impatience. The request for expulsion was repeated and accompanied by copies of a pamphlet written by Obregón Silva entitled *Las Cosas de Venezuela,* and of an article by Level de Goda with the title "Venezuela y Guzmán Blanco".[90] Later, several copies of *El Observador,* also published in Curaçao, were added to provide the necessary proof for the accusation.

It is not understood how the Attorney General of Curaçao before the second Venezuelan demand, could not have known about these publications. It almost leads one to believe that the colonial authorities in effect tried to protect conspiring refugees. This time there was no escape. The governor was advised to expel Level de Goda and to give Obregón Silva a stiff warning. Acting again in a "courteous and moderate manner",[91] he wrote Caracas

> "that Curaçao had never been wanting in its international relations with the Republic of Venezuela ... that in regard to the publications of Silva, although insulting toward the President of the Republic, they could not be considered as calculated to create a revolution ... and that they in no way made him liable for expulsion." [92]

Refusing compliance with this detail of the Venezuelan request the governor acknowledged that Level de Goda had been found guilty of endangering the peace of Venezuela and was ordered to leave the island.[83] No proof of any incriminating act was found nor given to implicate Díaz and Moreno, but the stiff warning was also extended to them. Venezuela's commercial agent, Boye, expressed meager appreciation for this action, but declared officially that the Governor of Curaçao had done "his duty of neutrality" in this case.[84]

This ultimatum delivered to Obregón, Silva and Moreno had no effect. Rafael Seijas, the new more intransigent Venezuelan Minister of Foreign Affairs, following a line of continuously applied pressure sent the Curaçao governor two new copies of El Observador which brutally criticized Guzmán Blanco and his regime. The articles were undoubtedly eye-openers, especially the one entitled "Gran Reparto" by Moreno who had acquired a deserved reputation as a man who did not tell fairy tales. Guzmán Blanco "as usual" had distributed the contents of the national treasury among those on whose support he counted for an eventual return, Moreno wrote. Among these supporters were the provisional president, Hermógenes López, the former Foreign Minister, Juan Bautista Urbaneja, and the president of the Senate, Nicolás Gil, called by Moreno "miserable beggars".[95] Obregón Silva, also ignoring the warning, continued his anti-guzmancista prose in an article entitled "Los Beduinos en Paris". Both he and Moreno were ordered to leave the colony. Again Díaz escaped expulsion.[96]

Venezuela's threat that "should no attention be paid to her demands, the government would be obliged to suspend what was still left of the commercial relations between the republic and the colony," alerted the American minister resident in Caracas. The Caribbean had long been included in the United States' "immediate sphere of interests". Trade with Venezuela, for instance, was important to U.S. merchants who controlled (in 1885) over 40 per cent of all imports and exports. "If Venezuela carries out her threat and closes her ports to all trafic," he wrote to the Secretary of State, "it will seriously affect and damage American commerce, as the Red D. Line, an American enterprise, does nine-tenths of the carrying trade between this country and the United States." [97]

But this time Guzmán Blanco's bite was not worse than his bark. The United States government ordered its minister in Caracas to inform the authorities of the United States' position. She

"would view with great concern such a measure as that indicated in your dispatch, whereby the ports of Venezuela might be closed to the produce and merchandise of the United States destined for Venezuela and transshipped *en route* in the port of Curaçao from one American vessel to another."

In rather strong words the consequences of Venezuelan policy were exposed:

"To suspend all sorts of commercial relations between her territory and that of the neighboring Dutch colonies would be a subject of deep and legitimate concern if its effects were to suspend commercial intercourse between the United States and Venezuela, and in such a case could not fail to provoke earnest remonstrance and suggest undesirable countervailing measures if insisted upon."

With the usual diplomatic niceties the provisional president López promptly assured President Cleveland that "the bonds of friendship which unite our two countries" together with "the best wishes for the uninterrupted prosperity and progress of the United States of America" were foremost in his mind. This assurance determined the policy the Venezuelan government proposed to follow after Guzmán Blanco's permanent departure in 1888 — one of leaving the matter as it stood.[98]

The Illustrious American never returned to his country, remaining in his beloved Paris. He made a few efforts as minister plenipotentiary to negotiate some deals for his country and perhaps Curaçao was part of them, but they did not affect the island. His role had ended and the only thing left to him was to write his memoirs. Smuggling continued to an unknown extent. Under successive presidents relations between Curaçao and Venezuela did not change and the almost traditional incidents continued to occur. In 1893, Crespo tried to reinstate the 30 per cent differential duties in their original harshness, but immediate American protests were again instrumental in cancelling this project.[99]

Diplomatic relations were finally restored in 1894 when Francisco Tosta García, Crespo's representative to The Hague, and Dutch Foreign Minister Jean Roëll signed an agreement for their normalization. For the first time in history the Dutch government, concerned about the colony's opinion in this negotiation, asked for it and received a favorable reaction. Both sides made concessions. Without admitting that her reclamations of 1875 were unrealistic and perhaps somewhat inflated, Venezuela was willing to abstain from those demands, while the Netherlands promised to do all in her power to stop exiles in Curaçao from conspiring against Caracas.[100] The continuous friction on the most evident cause of disruption seemed to have come to an end. Again as in 1872 the real issues, the principle of free trade and of free press, did not enter the debate.

16. CONCLUSION

This study has examined Curaçao's political relations with Venezuela under the Guzmán Blanco regime. The author has explored this uneasy relationship within the framework of the gradual development of political and economic contacts between colonial Curaçao and the Land of Bolívar. Venezuelans' increasing consciousness of what they considered to be their basic rights were obstructed by an outpost of rigid European colonialism uncomfortably close to their coasts. While the Great Liberal's arrogant pretensions gave this conflict its peculiar profile, they had little to do with liberal principles. Yet Guzmán Blanco's eighteen years in power certainly reflected growth in the political maturity of his country.

As for the island, its status as a colony was not to change for many years to come. The attitude of The Hague toward its problems, nevertheless, in the course of time underwent a slight change. In 1870 the Minister for the Colonies ordered the expulsion of Venezuelan refugees from the island against the advice of its governor and the outspoken protest of the Colonial *Raad*. A request of prominent citizens to undo what they considered a fatal decision was rebuffed. His Majesty was not at all pleased with this interference in an international question, the Minister for the Colonies answered the petitioners rather sarcastically.[1] A second petition protesting forced retirement of Governor De Rouville met a similar fate.[2] Both protests and the attitude of the Colonial *Raad* were, however, clear symptoms of an awakening sense of responsibility among Curaçao's residents.

Another sign of this awakening was the appearance of several weekly newspapers, in which the *vox populi* —in so far as we may consider the literate white and coloured upper classes as representative of the people — could express themselves more openly than in the *Curaçaosche Courant,* which evolved in the direction of an official island gazette. The most outspoken of these papers, *El Imparcial* and the *Civilisadó,* were mentioned above. They were short-lived, it is true, but they were, undoubtedly, exponents of that increasing dissatisfaction at being treated as minors, at being manipulated, and at being ruled without any say in one's own affairs.

A further step toward Curaçao's political maturity — under the growing threat of being bartered away to Venezuela — was A. M. Chumaceiro's pamphlet, *Is Curaçao te koop?* (Is Curaçao for Sale?). "If the Curaçao colony," he wrote, "had had more self-government than it has at present, much that has gone wrong would have been completely different." The Colonial *Raad* is not an elective body, he protested. It selects its own candidates, of which His Majesty — through the Minister for the Colonies — chooses some, while five of its thirteen members are direct appointees. What could be expected from such a legislative body?

> "New forces, summoned by free elections, brought into the Colonial *Raad* would undoubtedly be of great benefit and call into existence a new set of regulations which would coincide with local interests without hurting those of the Netherlands. And the Dutch government, in that case, should have more considerations for the feelings of this *Raad* than is now the case; it should trust that *Raad,* and bear in mind that it cannot judge questions more aptly than those who are on the spot." [3]

Chumaceiro was not alone. Although it would require many more years to effectively change the island's colonial status, prophets of new things to come were already voicing their predictions. And when, finally, new negotiations between the Netherlands and Venezuela were initiated,[4] The Hague showed more understanding than ever before and established an official inquiry board to sound out Curaçao's opinion. Local residents, in the vast majority, favored resumption of normal diplomatic relations with Venezuela and were diametrically opposed to a renewal of the nefarious trade in war materiel.

The Dutch government, which for such a long time had heeded neither expert information nor realistic warnings, but rather had maintained a peculiar ability to act upon bad advice, finally became aware that the colony was maturing and declared itself prepared to listen to the local voice. After its headstrong attitude had aggravated the conflict with Venezuela almost to the point of war, this concession, small as it may seem, opened the door to more local control of island affairs. This was Curaçao's only real gain in a conflict in which it was the principal loser.

APPENDICES

Appendix 1

Protocol for restoration of diplomatic relations between The Netherlands and Venezuela, March 21, 1872.

Protocole

Les soussignés baron Gericke de Herwijnen, Ministre des Affaires Etrangères de Sa Majesté le Roi des Pays-Bas et Lucio Pulido, Envoyé de la République de Vénézuéla, en mission auprès du Gouvernement Néerlandais, se sont réunis aujourd'hui au Ministère des Affaires Etrangères à La Haye, dans le but d'arrêter définitivement les mesures pour le rétablissement des relations diplomatiques entre les deux Etats.

Monsieur Lucio Pulido, ayant exhibé les pleins pouvoirs qui lui ont été délivrés par son Gouvernement, a déclaré être autorisé en vertu de ses instructions et des dits pleins pouvoirs, à adhérer aux bases d'arrangement consignées dans la note qui lui a été remise par le Ministre des Affaires Etrangères des Pays-Bas en date du 27 Avril 1871, et dont le contenu textuel est comme suit:

"En présence de la répugnance invincible, contre la réintégration, même temporaire, de monsieur Rolandus, dans les fonctions de chargé d'affaires à Caracas, le Gouvernement des Pays-Bas a consenti, conformément à l'autorisation du Roi, à examiner s'il serait possible, d'accepter sous une autre forme la satisfaction, à laquelle il est en droit de s'attendre. Malgré qu'il ne puisse de son côté adopter sans regret la pensée d'un arrangement, dont la réintégration de monsieur Rolandus ne serait pas le point de départ, il consentirait néanmoins à admettre une solution basée sur les conditions suivantes:

Le Gouvernement de la République des Etats Unis de Vénézuéla enverra à La Haye un personnage d'un rang élevé, en qualité de plénipotenciaire, chargé de la mission spéciale, de demander le rétablissement des relations actuellement interrompues entre le Gouvernement des Pays-Bas et celui de la République.

Le texte de l'allocution que le Plenipotenciaire adressera au Roi dans l'audience qu'il sollicitera de Sa Majesté, sera préalablement communiqué au Ministre des Affaires Etrangères. Outre les explications satisfaisantes que contiendra cette allocution, elle exprimera tous les regrets du Gouvernement de la République, ainsi que son vif désir de voir rétablir les relations de bonne entente entre les deux Gouvernements et d'éviter tout ce qui pourrait les compromettre à l'avenir. Il va sans dire, que toute récrimination à l'égard de monsieur Rolandus doit être évitée.

Lorsqu'un nouveau chargé d'affaires des Pays-Bas près le Gouvernement de Vénézuéla aura été nommeé, il sera reçu avec les plus grands honneurs, compatibles avec son rang, et dans l'audience qui lui sera accordée pour remettre ses lettres de créance, des sentiments analogues à ceux qui auront été manifestés par le plenipotenciaire de Vénézuéla à La Haye lui seront exprimés."

En conséquence de ce qui précède monsieur Lucio Pulido a remis à monsieur le baron Gericke de Herwijnen copie des lettres qui l'accréditent en qualité d'envoyé extraordinaire et ministre plenipotenciaire de la République des Etats Unis de Vénézuéla auprès de Sa Majesté le Roi des Pays-Bas, en vue de remplir la mission ci-dessus specifiée.

Le Ministre des Affaires Etrangères s'est engagé à soumettre l'accord ainsi établi à l'approbation du Roi et à demander, dans le plus bref délai possible, les ordres de Sa Majesté quant à l'audience à accorder à monsieur Lucio Pulido, afin de présenter ses lettres de créance et de s'acquitter de la mission qui lui est confiée.

En foi de quoi, le présent protocole a été dressé et signé en double original à La Haye, le 21 Mars mil huit cent soixante douze.

(signé) L. Gericke   (signé) Lucio Pulido

Appendix 2

Protocol signed in The Hague on August 20, 1894, to restore diplomatic relations between The Netherlands and Venezuela.

Protocole

Le Gouvernement de Sa Majesté la Reine des Pays-Bas et le Gouvernement des Etats Unis de Vénézuéla, étant tous deux animés du sincère désir de rétablir les relations diplomatiques entre les deux Pays sont convenus de ce qui suit:

Les réclamations formulées de part et d'autre, en 1875, donnèrent lieu à cette époque à une discussion, qui n'a malheureusement pu aboutir et que s'est terminée par la rupture des relations diplomatiques.

Depuis lors, les Pays-Bas et Vénézuéla, étant entrés dans la voie des concessions mutuelles, ont de leur propre gré supprimé toutes les causes de divergence entre les deux Pays.

De son côté le Gouvernement de la Reine constate, qu'il s'est empressé de communiquer au Gouvernement Vénézuélien, dans sa depêche du 6 juilliet 1889, le résultat de l'enquête rigoureuse à laquelle il fut officiellement procédé à Curaçao, relativement aux faits qui avaient provoqué les réclamations sousmentionnées des Etats Unis de Vénézuéla.

Quant au Gouvernement Vénézuélien, sans admettre nullement que ses réclamations ne fussent pas fondées, et sans vouloir, par cela, établir un précédent qui pourrait être invoqué à l'avenir, concède à ne plus insister sur les demandes antérieures.

Or les motifs de désaccord n'existant donc plus actuellement et les deux Gouvernements étant animés du vif désir d'écarter tout ce qui serait de nature à entraver le rétablissement immédiat des relations diplomatiques, malheureusement interrompues à la suite d'événements éloignés dont le souvenir tend à s'effacer complètement, sont convenus de clore definitivement la discussion et l'examen de toutes les anciennes questions en litige.

En outre, le Gouvernement Néerlandais, désirant donner au Gouvernement Vénézuélien une preuve de la vive satisfaction que lui cause la haute mission amicale de Monsieur le Général Francisco Tosta García manifeste de nouveau son intention d'empêcher par tous les moyens en son pouvoir tout complot, atteinte ou autre acte contraire à l'ordre public au Vénézuéla, dérogeant aux principes de la plus stricte neutralité envers le Gouvernement constitué du dit Pays, conformément aux règles établies par le droit des gens, et il renouvellera en ce sens aux autorités de ses Colonies de Curaçao, Bonaire, Aruba, St. Martin, St. Eustache et Saba les instructions formelles existant à cet effet.

En conséquence les soussignés, le jonkheer Jean Roëll, Ministre des Affaires Etrangères de Sa Majesté la Reine des Pays-Bas, et Monsieur le Général Francisco Tosta García, délégué spécial du Gouvernement des Etats-Unis de Vénézuéla, dûment autorisés par Sa Majesté la Reine Régénte du Royaume et par le Gouvernement des Etats-Unis de Vénézuéla ont opposé leurs signatures au présent protocole; lequel sera soumis à la ratification des pouvoirs compétents.

Fait en double, à La Haye le 20 août 1894.

(signé) J. Roëll   (signé) F. T. García

ABBREVIATIONS *

VZ   Venezolaanse Zaken (Venezuelan Affairs), the collection A-128 in *ARA* (Algemeen Rijks Archief, The Hague).

CD   Correspondencia diplomática, vol. I (1857-1904). A subcollection of the Holanda dossier of *MRE* (Ministerio de Relaciones Exteriores, Caracas).

CI   Cortesía internacional (idem).

FDdV   Funcionarios diplomáticos de Venezuela, 2 vols. (idem).

FDeV   Funcionarios diplomáticos en Venezuela (idem).

GQH   Gestiones, Quejas y Reclamaciones de Holanda, 17 vols. (idem).

GQV   Gestiones, Quejas y Reclamaciones de Venezuela (idem).

IRD   Interrupción de relaciones diplomáticas, 1870-72 (idem).

PHV   Pretensiones de Holanda contra Venezuela, 1875 (idem).

SP   Seguridad pública, vols. V-IX (1872-1908, (idem).

TC   Tratados y convenios, vol. II ,1861-1908 (idem).

CC   De Curaçaosche Courant.

GG   F. González Guinán, *Historia contemporánea de Venezuela*.

GO   Gaceta Oficial.

HTK   Handelingen van de Tweede Kamer der Staten Generaal.

KV   Koloniale Verslagen.

LA   Libro Amarillo.

NS   Nederlandse Staatscourant.

ON   La Opinión Nacional.

PB   Publicatie Blad.

WIG   West Indische Gids.

NWIG   Nieuwe West Indische Gids.

---

*   Most references are given in shortened form. For full titles we refer to the bibliography.

NOTES

CHAPTER 1

1 *NS*, 145, June 22, 1870.
2 Cornelis Ch. Goslinga, "Papachi Sassen", *NWIG* (1968), p. 108.
3 Rafael R. Castellanos, *Guzmán Blanco íntimo* (Caracas, 1969), pp. 77-78, letter of Antonio Guzmán B. to his wife, Ana Teresa, Curaçao, Sept. 8, 1869.
4 Castellanos, p. 73 writes that the oldest partner of the firm, Abraham J. Jesurun, did not want Guzmán Blanco and his party to embark in the *Midas* fearing official reprisals. He was negotiating with the Blue government.
5 *CC*, Febr. 19, 1870.
6 Information for this chapter was taken from a contra-memorandum of Wagner, the Governor of Curaçao, refuting a note of A. L. Guzmán, Aug. 12, 1870. This contra-memorandum is not dated.

CHAPTER 2

1 Theo P. M. de Jong, *De krimpende horizon van de Hollandse kooplieden* (Assen, 1966), pp. 61, 62, 75, 78, *et passim.*
2 This is stated in Report Kikkert "Curaçao in 1817" published by J. de Hullu in vol. 67 of the *Bijdragen tot de Taal-, Land- en Volkenkunde van Nederlandsch Indië* (1913), pp. 562-609. See also *CC,* Jan. 13, 1827.
3 Theo P. M. de Jong, "Nederland en Latijns Amerika", *Economisch Historisch Jaarboek*, XXIX (1963), pp. 18-20.
4 Karel H. Corporaal, *De internationaalrechtelijke betrekkingen tusschen Nederland en Venezuela*, 1816-1920 (Leiden, 1920), pp. 7-8.
5 This treaty is published in *Tratados públicos y acuerdos internacionales de Venezuela*, 1820-1900 (Caracas, 1951), 2nd ed., I, pp. 58-65.
6 *Ibid.,* pp. 79-81; 56-58; 91-104.
7 Amry van den Bosch, *Dutch Foreign Policy Since 1815* (The Hague, 1959), p. 213.
8 They are, like all colonial laws and regulations, published in a so-called *Publicatie Blad* (*PB*) followed by the year and a number. Dealing with this subject are *PB* 1822, no. 54; 1854, no. 17; 1858, no. 6.

CHAPTER 3

1 Goslinga, *loc. cit.,* p. 106.
2 *VZ*, Rolandus to Dutch For. Min., Aug. 9, 1869; Sept. 7, 1869, and a letter of the Dipl. Corps to Ven. For. Min., Aug. 10, 1869, and Aug. 20, 1869. Rolandus had not only tried to unite those nations whose subjects had claims against the Venezuelan government, but at the same time had given damaging evidence of conspiracy against the Ven. government by the exiles in Curaçao through intercepted letters.

3 The political relationship was similar to that of the British West Indian Crown colonies.

4 Castellanos, p. 80. Guzmán Blanco to his wife, Ana Teresa, Curaçao, Sept. 15, 1869: "Es un tormento vivir en este pontón con quince días sin una carta tuya . . ."

5 *GG*, IX, 245. Tello became the father-in-law of Venezuela's most famous nineteenth century painter, Arturo Michelena.

6 Castellanos, p. 99. Guzmán Blanco to Ana Teresa, Curaçao, Oct. 11, 1869: "Yo no me ocupo más que de la revolución, no veo sino a hombres que la sirven y me ayudan, no conosco sino del mismo asunto, ni estoy sino en casa con mi padre y Juan de Mata, y los amigos revolucionarios que vienen a revolucionar."

7 Originally published in Curaçao. The three parts are dated Oct. 20, 1869, Dec. 7, 1869, and Jana 1, 1870. Reproduced in *La doctrina liberal. Antonio Leocadio Guzmán*, vol. II in *Pensamiento político venezolano del siglo XIX*, series 6 (Caracas, 1961), pp. 161-356.

8 Goslinga, *loc. cit.*, p. 109. Address dated Febr. 6, 1870. The king refused.

9 *CC*, Febr. 5, 1870. This was said by Nicolaas Rojer. He was the father-in-law of the Venezuelan general Jorge Southerland (or Sutherland) who had a plantation at Piscadera Bay, Curaçao.

10 Goslinga, *loc. cit.*, p. 110. De Rouville to Min. of Col., Febr. 18, 1870.

11 *Ibid.*, p. 111. Min. of Col. to De Rouville, May 30, 1870.

CHAPTER 4

1 *GG*, IX, 289: ". . . por la intimidación que le hizo la autoridad colonial."

2 R. A. Rondón Márquez, *Guzmán Blanco, el autócrata civilizador* (Caracas, 1944), II, 129. See also Felipe Larrazábal, *Ideario político y económico* (Caracas, 1963), pp. 153-54.

3 *CC*, April 9, 1870.

4 *CC*, June 25, 1870.

5 *IRD*, 1-9. See also *GG*, IX, 343. A. L. Guzmán "declaró que éste Rolandus era un ministre impossible para la buena armonía que Venezuela deseaba mantener con el gobierno de los Países Bajos." See also Parra, *Doctrinas*, I, 99; and *LA*, 1882, II, 259-77, 284-86.

6 *KV*, 1871, Bijlage 1871/72, p. 487. Rolandus sailed first to Río de la Hacha and from there to Willemstad. In the summer of 1872 he returned to the Netherlands. See also Corporaal, p. 241.

7 *NS*, June 22, 1870, no. 145. See also *GG*, IX, 343.

8 *IRD*, 1-10; *VZ*, Guzmán to Dutch Foreign Min., May 22, 1870.

9 *HTK*, II, 1869/70, pp. 1776-79. See also *NS*, June 22, 1870, no. 145, and *GG*, IX, 349-50.

10 Corporaal, pp. 171-79.

11 John de Pool, *Del Curaçao que se va* (Santiago de Chile, 1935), pp. 334-35.

12 Isaac S. and Suzanne A. Emmanuel, *History of the Jews of the Netherlands Antilles* (Cincinnati, 1970), II, Appendix 3, pp. 734-36. The *Honfleur* measured 169 tons, the *Sarah* 44.

13 *Ibid.*, I, 360-61.

14 *VZ*, Dutch For. Min. to the king, June 11, 1870. In reality there were two notes of that date: one about the seizure of the *Honfleur*, the second asking the recall of Rolandus.

15 *VZ*, Dutch For. Min. to the king, June 16, 1870.

16   *NS*, June 22, 1870, no. 145.
17   *Ibid.*
18   *HTK*, II, 1870/71, p. 34.
19.   *VZ*, Dutch For. Min. to Ven. For. Min., June 28, 1870.
20   *HTK*, II, 1870/71, p. 34.
21   *VZ*, Dutch For. Min. to Ven. For. Min., June 28, 1870.

CHAPTER 5

1   *HTK*, II, Bijlage 1870/71, no. 70, 2.
2   *Ibid.*, no. 70, 5: 4 paragraphs, 51 complaints. These complaints are also found in *GQV*. Ven. note is dated Aug. 12, 1870.
3   Corporaal, pp. 249-73.
4   *VZ*, Contra-memorandum of Wagner, June 21, 1871, received in The Hague, July 19, 1871. Wagner added to this complaint that Rolandus had informed him of the developments in Caracas in two official letters, dated March 29, and May 11, 1870.
5   *VZ*, Willem Sassen to the Gov. of Curaçao, June 25, 1870, and Wagner's answer, June 25, 1870.
6   Corporaal, p. 264. Articles 23 and 24 of the treaty of 1830 between the Netherlands and Venezuela included an arrangement in terms of consular representation. But these articles did not apply to the Dutch West Indian colonies (Corporaal, p. 114). See also W. J. M. van Eysinga, *Proeve eener inleiding tot het Nederlandsch tractatenrecht* (Leiden, 1907), p. 118; and Parra, *Doctrinas*, I, 53-54. Mendes was commercial agent, not consul.
7   Corporaal, pp. 269-70.
8   The available material in *GQV* and *VZ* (1870-71) is almost identical. The documents are also translated and published in *HTK*, II, Bijlage 1870/71, no. 70, 1-7. See also *GG*, IX, 349-50.
9   *VZ*, Guzmán to Dutch For. Min., Aug. 12, 1870, an answer to the Dutch note of June 28, 1870. See also Wagner's contra-memorandum, June 21, 1871, and *HTK*, II, Bijlage 1870/71, 1-7.
10   *VZ*, Wagner to Min. of Col., Jan. 21, 1871.
11   *PB*, 1871, 3.
12   Imprisonment from 1 to 6 months and/or a fine of 25 to 300 guilders.
13   *VZ*, Min. of Col. to Wagner, Febr. 28, 1871.
14   *VZ*, Sassen to Wagner, Nov. 27, 1870.
15   *Ibid.*
16   *VZ*, Report of Captain A. Topete of the Spanish man-of-war *Vasco Núñez de Balboa* in the port of Willemstad, Nov. 26, 1870. See also Wagner to Min. of Col., Dec. 7, 1870.
17   Emmanuel, I, 361.
18   *VZ*, Wagner to Min. of Col., Dec. 21, 1870.
19   Emmanuel, I, 446.
20   *VZ*, Request dated Jan. 4, 1871. *La Gracia de Dios* measured 17 tons and was seized Dec. 20.
21   *VZ*, Wagner to Min. of Col., Jan. 21, 1871.
22   *VZ*, Wagner received two letters dated March 17 and 23. See also R. la Roche to Wagner, April 17, 1871. Roche was the commander of the Ven. man-of-war *Apostadero*.
23   *VZ*, Wagner to Min. of Col., Febr. 22, 1871. Ortega presented himself Febr. 7.

24 *VZ*, Mendes to Wagner, Jan. 13, 1871.
25 *VZ*, Guzmán to Wagner, Jan. 25, 1871.
26 See for these complaints and for many more *VZ*, Guzmán to the President
   of the State Falcón, March 17, 1871, and Wagner to Guzmán, July 19, 1871.
27 For more extensive information, *GQV*, *passim*.
28 *VZ*, Guzmán to Wagner, March 17, 1871.
29 *VZ*, Wagner to Min. of Col., March 30, 1871.
30 *VZ*, Wagner to Min. of Col., May 22, 1871.
31 *VZ*, Report of F. L. Geerling, Commander of H. M. *Admiraal van Wassenaar*, Oct. 28, 1870: "The island ... divided into two camps, the Blues and
   the Yellows .... Many have outspoken sympathy for the present government
   of Venezuela." The firms of Jeudah Senior and A. J. Jesurun & Son favored
   the Blues; other merchants like Hendrick Evertsz, Genereux de Lima, and
   Jacob R. Mendes followed the Yellows.
32 *VZ*, Min of Col. to Dutch For. Min., March 22, 1871. Rolandus had not
   even protested.
33 *VZ*, Wagner to Min. of Col., May 22, 1871. Pulgar's letter is dated May 6.
   No proof was found but suspicion remained.
34 *VZ*, Wagner to Min. of Col., Sept. 22, 1871.
35 *VZ*, Guzmán to Wagner, Oct. 30, 1871; Wagner to Min. of Col., Nov. 18,
   1871.
36 *VZ*, Wagner to Min. of Col., March 21, 1872.
37 *VZ*, Dutch For. Min. to Min. of Col., July 12, 1871.
38 *VZ*, Dutch For. Min. to Rolandus, May 31, 1872.
39 *VZ*, Wagner to Min. of Col., June 10, 1872.

CHAPTER 6

1 *IRD*, folios 1-10 *et passim*. *VZ*, Guzmán to Wagner, Aug. 19, 1871.
2 *VZ*, Min. of Col. to Dutch For. Min., Febr. 4 and 24, 1871.
3 *VZ*, Pulido to Dutch For. Min., Febr. 24, April 18, 1871.
4 From April 19, 1871 to March 27, 1872.
5 Corporaal, Bijlage 31, pp. 617-19: "... en présence de la répugnance invincible contre la réintégration ... même temporaire, de M. Rolandus." See
   also *HTK*, II, 1872/73, p. 389; and *NS*, March 31, 1872, no. 78.
6 Corporaal, p. 618: "Il sera reçu avec les plus grands honneurs, compatibles
   avec son rang, et dans l'audience qui lui sera accordé ... des sentiments
   analogues à ceux qui auront été manifestés par le plénipotenciaire à La Haye
   lui seront exprimés."
7 *HTK*, II, 1872/73, p. 155. One of the most arduous defenders of these claims
   and an outspoken critic of the Minister of Foreign Affairs was D. van Eck,
   a lawyer and member of the Second Chamber of the States General who
   at the time had been hired by the Jesurun House to protect its interests.
   See *VZ*, Van Eck to Dutch For. Min., Sept. 11, 1871.
8 *TC*, II, 107. See also E. G. Lagemans, *Recueil des traités* (La Haye, 1873),
   VI, 414-15; Corporaal, p. 619; and Appendix I.
9 *FDdV*, I, 106, 124, Pulido to Guzmán, March 29, April 13, 1872.
10 *CC*, Sept. 28, 1872.
11 *VZ*, Instruction to Brakel, April, 1872.
12 *VZ*, Brakel to Dutch For. Min., Aug. 21, 1872.
13 *VZ*, Brakel to Dutch For. Min., Sept. 7, 1872. Brakel also mentions

another merchant, M. D. Jesurun, whose identiy could not be established.
14 *FDeV*, 96, Guzmán to Gericke, Sept. 24, 1872.
15 *FDeV*, 101, with description of Brakel's reception. See also *VZ*, Brakel to Dutch For. Min., Sept. 21, 1872; and *ON*, Sept. 14, 1872.

CHAPTER 7

1   Emmanuel, I, 349. See also Parra, *Doctrinas*, I, 298-300.
2   *LA*, 1856, pp. 31-32; Corporaal, pp. 171-72.
3   Emmanuel, I, 350. Titles of the pamphlets: *La Mano de Dios, El Pueblo y los Judíos, A los Judíos, El Pueblo*. See also Parra, *Doctrinas*, I, 298-300.
4   *Tratados públicos*, I, 207-209. Emmanuel, I, 351.
5   *HTK*, II, Bijlage 1863/64, p. 359.
6   *CC*, Oct. 29, 1864.
7   *CC*, June 2, 1866.
8   De Pool, pp. 327, 334-35.
9   Corporaal, p. 215: "Door deze transactie werd het geldelijk belang der firma ten nauwste met de gang van zaken in Venezuela verbonden."
10 Research did not reveal much of importance regarding Pardo's claims. Perhaps he was the Isaac Pardo who was co-founder of a masonic lodge in Caracas and secretary of the Grant Order of Venezuela in 1866. See *El Espejo Masónico* (New York, 1867), II, 224 and 288, as quoted by Emmanuel, I, 368.
11 Manuel Briceño, *Los 'ilustres' o la estafa de los Guzmanes*, 3rd ed. (Caracas, n.y.), p. 70. A first edition was published in Curaçao in 1883. See also L. Level de Goda, *Historia contemporánea de Venezuela, política y militar*, 2nd ed., (Caracas, 1954), pp. 608-9.
12 *Tratados públicos*, I, 280-83; 293-94; 302; 302-6. This work does not contain the agreement with Spain which is found in *Colección de los tratados de paz, alianza, comercio, etc. ajustados por la Corona de España con las potencias extranjeras, desde el reinado del Señor Don Felipe Quinto hasta el presente* (Madrid, 1796-1890), IV, 173-74.
13 Corporaal, pp. 216-17.
14 *Ibid.*, pp. 281-82.
15 *VZ*, Correspondence of Rolandus with Dutch For. Min. during the year 1869.
16 *VZ*, Dutch ambassador in London to For. Min., Sept. 20, 1871.
17 *VZ*, Wagner to Min. of Col., Nov. 22, 1871, and memorandum of the Diplomatic Corps signed by M. Llorente Vásquez (Spain), R. J. C. Middleton (Great Britain), G. B. Viviani (Italy), Von Gülick (German Empire), and G. Sturup (Denmark). The U.S.A. did not join, neither did the Netherlands.
18 *VZ*, Guzmán to Dutch For. Min., Dec. 4, 1871. See for a summary of Guzmán Blanco's financial manipulations, George S. Wise, *Caudillo. A Portrait of Antonio Guzmán Blanco* (New York, 1951), pp. 145-60, chapter IX: Financial Chicanery.
19 *VZ*, Envoy to Dutch For. Min., March 22, 1872.
20 *VZ*, Dutch envoy in Washington to Dutch For. Min., May 7, 1872. The envoy called this offer 'a broad application of the Monroe Doctrine' (eene uitgestrekte toepassing van den regel van Monroe).
21 *VZ*, Brakel to For. Min., Sept. 2, 1872: "... overigens ben ik van het gevoelen van de V. S. minister alhier, dat die tijdelijke verwisseling van personen voor onze belangen nadeelig is."

22 *Ibid.*
23 *GG,* X, 120.
24 *GO,* Dec. 18, 1872.
25 *VZ,* Brakel to Dutch For. Min., Sept. 25, 1872. Since 1863 the U.S. reclamations amounted to 200,000 *pesos* although Venezuela recognized only 80,000 to 100,000 (see *GG,* X, 60) as legitimate. Pile seems to have suggested a kind of sliding scale which looks as follows:

For the first year:

Of each 100 *pesos*:	for government expenses	$ 60
	for public debts	34
	for dipl. claims	6
		$ 100

For the second year:

Of each 100 *pesos*:	for government expenses	$ 55
	for public debts	38,25
	for dipl. claims	6,75
		$ 100

For the third and following years:

Of each 100 *pesos*:	for government expenses	$ 50
	for public debts	42,50
	for dipl. claims	7,50
		$ 100

26 *VZ,* Brakel to Dutch For. Min., Sept. 25, 1872.
27 Corporaal, p. 283.
28 *Ibid.*
29 *CD,* I, 29 ff. gives the correspondence on these claims between Brakel and Barrios. The same information is found in *VZ.* See especially Brakel to Dutch For. Min., Sept. 23, 1872.
30 *Ibid.* The new claims were specified as follows:

For the *Honfleur*:	wages and maintenance	10,400 *ven.*	
	insurance	2,800	
	subsidies	9,600	
	damages to cargoes	8,500	
	damages to mail contract	8,700	
	value decrease	20,000	
			60,000 *ven.*
For the *Sarah*:	wages and maintenance	2,400 *ven.*	
	insurance, etc.	600	
	damages to cargoes	3,000	
	value decrease	4,000	
			10,000
Damages caused by the arrest of Mr. Jesurun		100,000 *ven.*	
losses for his firm		150,000	
			250,000
			320,000 *ven.*

31 *VZ*, Van Eck to Dutch For. Min., July 26, 1872.
32 *GG*, X, 139-40: "... los extranjeros que tomaron parte en las contiendas
    domésticas de los venezolanos perdían su carácter de neutralidad ... Los
    extranjeros domiciliados ni los transeuntes tenían derecho para occurrir a la
    vía diplomática sino cuando habienda agotado los recursos legales ... Reclama-
    ciones contra la nación por razón de daños, perjuicios, o expropriaciones por
    actos de empleados nacionales o de los estados ... debían hacerse por formal
    demanda ante la Alta Corte Federal." The former law, dated March 6, 1866,
    had stipulated quite differently: No foreigner has the right to claim com-
    pensation from the government of the republic for damages suffered as a
    result of political strife or other causes in as far as these damages are caused
    by legal authorities, except for always having the right to claim from third
    parties compensation for damages in accordance with the common law and
    what it describes.
33 *VZ*, Brakel to Dutch For. Min., July 21, 1873. In a letter dated June 24,
    1873, Brakel quotes Pile criticizing the paragraphs forbidding foreigners to
    invoke the intervention of their diplomatic representatives. Pile called articles
    8 and 9 "unexampled and arrogant."
34 *VZ*, Dutch envoy in Paris to For. Min., Apr. 20, 1873.
35 *VZ*, Dutch envoy in Rome to For. Min., May 20, 1873.
36 *ON*, Dec. 12, 1872. This article first appeared in the *Paris Journal*, Nov. 11,
    1872, signed by a certain Peña Villegas. See also *VZ*, Brakel to Dutch For.
    Min., Jan. 20, 1873.
37 *CD*, I, 29-32, Brakel to Barrios, Febr. 17 and 24, 1873; Barrios to Brakel,
    Febr. 19, 1873. See also *VZ*, Brakel to Dutch For. Min., June 20, 1873.
38 *VZ*, Report Rolandus, May 25, 1869.
39 *VZ*, Van Eck to Dutch For. Min., Nov. 8, 1872.
40 *VZ*, Brakel to Dutch For. Min., Jan. 19, 1874.
41 As summarized by Brakel, *VZ*, Brakel to Dutch For. Min., June 20, 1873.
    See also *ON*, June 14, 1873, and *GG*, X, 192.
42 *VZ*, Brakel to Dutch For. Min., July 2, 1873. The joint memorandum was
    signed by R. T. C. Middleton (Great Britain), C. B. Viviani (Italy), J.
    Brakel (the Netherlands), W. A. Pile (U.S.A.), and Ch. Goepp (German
    Empire). It was directed to J. M. Blanco, Venezuelan Minister of Foreign
    Affairs.
43 *VZ*, German envoy in The Hague to Dutch For. Min., May 17, 1871: "... il
    n'y a qu'un seul moyen pour sauvegarder les interêts des étrangers, savoir
    une démarche collective faite auprès du Gouvernement de la République par
    la majorité des puissances representées à Vénézuéla ... Une escuadre de la
    marine imperiale allemande ... se rendra en quelques semaines dans les eaux
    des Indes Occidentales ... Le Gouvernement Impérial Allemand se flatte
    de l'espoir que le Gouvernement Royal Néerlandais qui a déjà éprouvé l'in-
    efficacité des efforts isolés se trouvera d'accord avec lui et voudra consentir
    à ce que le chargé d'affaires de l'Empire Germanique à Caracas ... se joigne
    au nom du Gouvernement Royal Hollandais aux démarches collectives..."

CHAPTER 8

1 *VZ*, Dutch For. Min. to Min. of Col., May 4, 1872.
2 *VZ*, Barrios to Brakel, Nov. 20, 1872.
3 *VZ*, Brakel to Dutch For. Min., Dec. 2, 1872.

4   *Ibid.*, Senior's comment was from Jan. 15, 1870. Guzmán Blanco, for in-
    stance, left behind on Curaçao in 1870, an illegitimate son, Juan J. Guzmán.
5   *ON*, Jan. 21, 1873. In *El Liberal* of Jan. 9, 1873, he is called "el jefe de
    los chinqueros."
6   *CD*, I, 27, Barrios to Brakel, Dec. 12, 1872. The Hotel Americano burned
    down during the riots of May, 1969.
7   *ON*, Jan. 21, 1873, contains copies of the letters. See also *VZ*, Dutch For.
    Min. to Min. of Col., May 14, 1873.
8   *VZ*, Dutch For. Min. to Min. of Col., Jan. 23, 1873.
9   *VZ*, Protest of Pirela Sutil, dated Dec. 28, 1872. He received an extension
    until Jan. 8, 1873.
10 Robert L. Gilmore, *Caudillism and Militarism in Venezuela, 1810-1910*
    (Athens, Ohio, 1964), p. 81, note 36, mentions José Anicete Serrano as the
    author of a conservative pamphlet, *Violencia ejercida por el poder ejecutivo
    de la República de la Venezuela en 1848*, probably the cause of his expulsion.
    Sassen was the Attorney General who sided with De Rouville in the expul-
    sion question of 1870. See Goslinga, *loc. cit.*
11 Corporaal, p. 291, mentions a request of Serrano directed to the Second
    Chamber of the Dutch Parliament, dated Oct. 3, 1873, asking permission
    to return. It was refused on Wagner's advice.
12 *VZ*, Wagner to Min. of Col., Febr. 21, 1873.
13 *VZ*, Brakel to Wagner, Jan. 20, 1873.
14 *VZ*, Wagner to Min. of Col., Mar. 16, 1873.
15 *Ibid.*
16 *VZ*, Pulido to Dutch For. Min., June 11, 1873: "... que M. Brakel s'est
    fait une excellente position dans la bonne société de Caracas."
17 *CD*, I, 29-32, Brakel to Barrios, Febr. 17 and 24, 1873; Barrios to Brakel,
    Febr. 19, 1873. See also *VZ*, Brakel to Dutch For. Min., Febr. 20, 1873;
    Corporaal, p. 291, and *GO*, Febr. 15, 1873.

CHAPTER 9

1   *VZ*, Brakel to Dutch For. Min., Febr. 20, 1874.
2   *Ibid.* The ad was placed in *CC* of Jan. 8, 1874.
3   *VZ*, Blanco to Brakel, Febr. 21, 1874.
4   *VZ*, A. J. Jesurun to Dutch envoy in Paris, March 11, 1874: "... une
    nouvelle injustice de la part du gouvernement de Vénézuela ... le gouverne-
    ment a suspendu le payment de la misérable somme que l'on commença à
    me remettre."
5   *VZ*, Van Eck to Dutch For. Min., Mar. 18, 1874.
6   *VZ*, Brakel to Dutch For. Min., July 9, 1874.
7   *VZ*, Wagner to Min. of Col., Apr. 13, 1874. See also José F. Freyle, Consul
    of Venezuela in Río de la Hacha to Ven. For. Min., Jan. 29, 1874.
8   *VZ*, Mendes to Ven. For. Min., Febr. 6, 1874.
9   *VZ*, Wagner to Min. of Col., Apr. 13, 1874.
10 *Ibid.* See also note 6, chapter V, on the consular arrangements.
11 *VZ*, Brakel to Wagner, April 25, 1874.
12 *VZ*, Brakel to Dutch For. Min., Mar. 19, 1874.
13 *GO*, Nov. 16, 1875. Also Blanco to Brakel, Febr. 21, July 1, Aug. 20 and 27,
    1874; Wagner to Min. of Col., July 21, 1874; and Brakel to Blanco, Aug. 17,
    1874.

14 In 1824 differential rights were already levied by Gran Columbia to encourage direct trade with Europe and the United States. They were abolished in 1829 with the dissolution of Gran Colombia.
15 *VZ*, Wagner to Brakel, Sept. 28, 1874.
16 *VZ*, Wagner to Min. of Col., Sept. 30, 1874.
17 *VZ*, Brakel to Dutch For. Min., Oct. 14, 1874.
18 *VZ*, Dutch For. Min. to Brakel, Nov. 25, 1874.
19 *CC*, Nov. 7 and 14, 1874, Febr. 13, 1875. See also *VZ*, Correspondence of Brakel with Dutch For. Min., starting Oct. 28, 1874.
20 *CC*, Nov. 7 and 14, 1875.
21 *VZ*, Blanco to Brakel, Nov. 18, 1874.
22 *VZ*, Blanco to Brakel, Nov. 9, 1874.
23 *GO*, Nov. 19, 20, 22, 1875, contains the extensive *Resumen de pruebas que fundan y legitiman la reclamación de gastos y perjuicios que el Gobierno de los Estados de Venezuela entabla ante el Gobierna de S.M. el Rey de los Países Bajos*, Caracas, May 4, 1875, also in *VZ*, which has besides the Spanish original a French translation. This *Resumen* includes a summary of events of the year 1874 and 1875 up till May. Signed by Blanco. See also *GG*, X, 358.
24 The identity of this member could not be established.
25 *VZ*, Blanco to Brakel, Nov. 9, 1874.
26 *VZ*, Blanco to Brakel, Nov. 12, 1874; Brakel to Wagner, Nov. 13, 1874, and to Cornelis van Seypesteyn, Governor of Surinam.
27 *SP*, V, VI, gives abundant information from the Venezuelan point of view. See also *GO*, Jan. 30, and Nov. 16, 1875. Brakel had informed Blanco of Wagner's prerogatives to apply or suspend the Royal Decree of 1871 with his letter of Aug. 7, 1874. Justification of the seizure was given by the Venezuelan Fed. High Court decision of Jan. 26, 1875 (*GO*, Jan. 30, 1875).
28 This ship — or a ship with the same name — has played a role in Venezuelan history worth remembering. In the turbulent years of the Civil War of 1858-63, it had served as a blockade breaker when a squadron of General Páez closed the Lake of Maracaibo. In 1869, it had brought Guzmán Blanco and other fugitives to Curaçao. The *Resumen* (see note 23) includes the interrogation of all crew members.
29 The identity of Waldemar Worm could not be established.
30 *VZ, Resumen*, pp. 43-45. The ship they were awaiting on Barcelona's coast was the *Mary*, size unknown, owned by the Jesurun House.
31 *VZ, Resumen*, p. 43. The Captain, Rudolf D. Schoonewolf, the boatswain Alexander Wegman (also called Jan Hendrik Wegman), Waldemar Worm, and the crew were interrogated Nov. 9, 1874, and following days. The testimony of young Juan Rodríguez, age 12, was crucial to the Venezuelan case (*SP*, V, 83, Nov. 14, 1874). The official interpreter was a certain Isaac Pardo. It is not known if he was one of the Dutch claimants in the "diplomatic debts".
32 *VZ*, Protest of April 2, 1875, signed by Captain Schoonewolf and the crew members on their return to Curaçao after five months. The Second Chamber of the Dutch States General became involved in the scandal. The accusation of maltreatment was denied by Rojas and Blanco. See Wagner to Min. of Col., Apr. 6, 1875.
33 *SP*, V, 218-306, and *GO*, Nov. 16, 1875. See also *VZ*, Brakel to Blanco, Nov. 12, 14, and 16. 1874.
34 *VZ*, Brakel to Blanco, Nov. 27, 1874.
35 *VZ*, Jesurun to Wagner, Nov. 19, 1874.

36 *VZ*, Brakel to Dutch For. Min., Nov. 28, 1875. The local authorities referred Wagner to the government in Caracas.
37 *ON*, Dec. 5, 1874.
38 *VZ*, Wagner to Min. of Col., Dec. 8, 1874. The Dutch For. Min. stated his opinion clearly in his letters of December 4, 1874, to Wagner, Brakel, and the Commander of the Dutch squadron.

CHAPTER 10

1 *SP*, V, 218 ff., contains the correspondence between Brakel and Blanco on the *Midas*. See also *GO*, Nov. 16 and 17, 1875, and *VZ*, 1874 and 1875, with the correspondence between Dutch For. Min. to the Ministers of Col. and Marine, Brakel, Wagner, and the Commander of the squadron ready to leave for the Caribbean. The compensation, the Min. informed Brakel, could wait because of the political complications as long as the principle of an obligation was recognized.
2 *VZ*, Instruction for Commander Capellen, Jan. 14, 1975.
3 *VZ*, Blanco to Wagner, Jan. 13, 1875. Blanco assured Wagner that there were 6 blockading units at La Vela de Coro. One of them was the *Midas*, rechristened *Jesurum*.
4 *VZ, Resumen*, pp. 18-19.
5 *Ibid.*, p. 20. The identiy of this schooner could not be established. If it were the former *Elvira*, its size would be 45 tons and its owner the Jesurun House.
6 *Ibid.*
7 *Ibid.*, p. 19, one of the few cases in which the cargo was completely itemized:

> 1 chest with drums and horns
> 64 chests with each 25 pounds of gunpowder
> 124 barrels with each 25 pounds of gunpowder
> 30 chests with 2,000 leather strips
> 95 chests with 2,000 rifles
> 100 barrels with 100 quintals of lead in bars
> 20 barrels with 100 quintals lead bullets
> 5 barrels with 525,000 pistons
> 1 chest with 50 packages of paper
> 53 barrels with 1,060 rifles

8 *Ibid.* These facts, taken from the *Resumen* are substantiated by many witnesses.
9 The one mysterious detail is the identity of Waldemar Worm. He seems to have been a man without any means who hired himself out in this type of adventure.
10 *VZ, Resumen*, pp. 54 ff.
11 *GG*, X, 358: "Creyó el Gobierno que podía hacer reintegrar en la Tesorería Nacional la cantidad que correspondía a la legación, pero procediendo equitativamente, decidió que se aplicara a la amortización de las otras reclamaciones de súbditos holandeses que conservaban su carácter de neutrales."
12 *VZ*, Alejandro Goiticoa to Blanco, Nov. 27, 1874.
13 *ON*, Jan. 25, 1875.
14 *VZ*, Wagner to Min. of Col., Febr. 2, 1875. Henríquez deserted the *guzmancistas*.

15 *VZ*, Brakel to Blanco, Febr. 6, 1875.
16 *VZ*, Van Capellen to Brakel aboard H.M. Leeuwarden, Febr. 22, 1875. The Dutch men-of-war were badly needed in the Achinese war. Ven. reports on the *Midas* question are found in *SP*, V and VI.
17 *VZ*, Brakel to Van Capellen, Febr. 27, 1875.
18 *VZ*, Brakel to Wagner, Febr. 27, 1875.
19 *VZ*, Brakel to Dutch For. Min., Mar. 8, 1875.
20 *VZ*, Dutch For. Min. to envoys in London, Paris, Berlin, Madrid, Rome, and Washington, March 12, 1875.
21 *VZ*, Dutch envoy in London to Dutch For. Min., Mar. 16, 1875.
22 *VZ*, Brakel to Wagner, Febr. 27, 1875; Wagner to Brakel, Mar. 8, 1875.
23 *VZ*, Brakel to Dutch For. Min., Mar. 13, 1875.
24 Minister of the Colonies until 1876 was W. Baron van Goltstein.
25 *ON*, Mar. 12, 1875. In spite of the existing tensions the port officials permitted the crews to disembark and handed out passports for shore leave. *CI*, 17. Eee also *SP*, VI.
26 *VZ*, Wagner to Min. of Col., Apr. 3, 1875.

CHAPTER 11

1 *VZ*, Blanco to Wagner, Mar. 20, 1875; Wagner to Min. of Col., Apr. 3 and May 7, 1875.
2 *VZ*, Boye to Wagner, Apr. 21, 1875. Boye reported their activities to Blanco in several letters. See *CVeH*, VII, 28 *et passim*.
3 *VZ*, Wagner to Min. of Col., May 7, 1875.
4 *ON*, Apr. 13, 1875. The original Dutch version appeared in the *Dagblad van Zuid-Holland en 's-Gravenhage*, Jan. 26, 1875.
5 *VZ*, Blanco to Brakel, May 3, 1875. This note added to that list the names of J. G. Riera, R. Rivas, and P. Consuegra. Some time later José R. Henríquez, the editor of *El Imparcial*, was also added.
6 *GG*, X, 381.
7 *VZ*, Blanco to Dutch For. Min., May 4, 1875. See also *Vénézuéla et les Pays-Bas. Documents relatifs à la rupture des rapports officiels entre les gouvernements du Vénézuéla et des Pays-Bas* (Paris, 1875), pp. 4-11, presumably edited by Rojas. A Spanish version was published in Caracas in 1876. We refer to the French version as *Documents relatifs*.
8 *VZ*, Blanco to Dutch For. Min., May 4, 1875; *Documents relatifs*, pp. 4-11; *LA*, 1876, pp. 115 ff., and *FDdV*, I, 166 ff.
9 See on Rojas, *The Reluctant Diplomacy of José María Rojas*, unpublished doctoral dissertation by William L. Harris, University of Florida (Gainesville, 1973) and José M. de Rojas, *Recuerdos de la patria* (Caracas, 1963), pp. 55-60.
10 *GQH*, XII, 134-39 gives the correspondence between Brakel and Blanco. See also *FDdV*, I, 163 ff.
11 *FDdV*, I, 163, Blanco to Rojas, May 4, 1875.
12 William L. Harris, *The Reluctant Diplomacy of José María Rojas, 1873-1883*, Chapter II. See also *FDdV*, I, 177-78.
13 *FDdV*, I, 185, Rojas to Blanco, June 3, 1875. See also *Recuerdos*, p. 55.
14 *FDdV*, I, 188 ff.: "Minutas de la conferencia celebrada hoy 4 de junio á las cuatro de la tarde con el Ministro de Relaciones Exteriores en su despacho," and *VZ*, Report Dutch For. Min. to Cabinet, June 5, 1875.

15 *VZ*, Pulido to Dutch For. Min., June 5, 1875.
16 *VZ*, Dutch For. Min. to the king, June 18, 1875.
17 *VZ*, Dutch For. Min. to Min. of Col., June 17, 1875.
18 *Recuerdos*, pp. 57-58. The conversation was short and held in French. The Rojas later commented: "A mi me pareció que el rey no estaba *half and a-half*, sino mucho más avanzado, *three quarters and three quarters*," referring to a play of words by Agrícollar and meaning that William III was only half pleasant in the late afternoon. Rojas seemed to have met the king when the latter was in a bad mood.
19 *VZ*, Dutch For. Min. to the king, June 18, 1875. See also J. Woltring, ed., *Bescheiden betreffende de buitenlandse politiek van Nederland, 1848-1919*, vol. II ('s-Gravenhage, 1965), pp. 128-30. In *MRE* information was found in *FDdV*, I, 166 *et passim*; *SP*, V and VI, *et passim*. See also *LA*, 1876, pp. 80 ff. and *GO*, Nov. 18 and 22, 1875.
20 Harris suggests that Rojas viewed the entire proceeding as one of delay which is probably not true. See *Reluctant Diplomacy*, chapter III.
21 *VZ*, Dutch For. Min. to the king, July 2, 1875.
22 Woltring, II, 138-42.
23 *Ibid*.
24 *VZ*, Rojas to Dutch For. Min., July 19, 1875: ". . . le plus profond étonnement en prenant connaissance d'une décision si exceptionellement grave." See also *LA*, 1876, p. 127, and *GO*, Nov. 23, 1875.
25 *PHV*, folio 2, Rojas to Blanco, July 8, 1875.
26 *VZ*, Dutch For. Min. to Brakel, July 27, 1875. Curiously enough Rojas received similar instruction from Blanco in case the Dutch refused the Ven. claims, *FDdV*, I, 246.
27 *FDdV*, I, 230, Blanco to Brakel, June 26, 1875. See also *VZ*, Brakel to Dutch For. Min., June 21, 1875.
28 *Ibid*. See also Blanco to Brakel, July 3, 1875.
29 *VZ*, Wagner to Min. of Col., Aug. 10, 1875. This manifesto, dated June 8, 1875, was printed in Curaçao by the Imprenta del Comercio and from there distributed.
30 *FDdV*, I, 233 ff., Blanco to Rojas, July 13, 1875; Rojas to Blanco, July 10, 1875; *VZ*, Blanco to Brakel, July 3, 1875.
31 *Gaceta Internacional*, V, 167, Aug. 2, 1875. p. 15. The time difference of only 9 days in both publications suggests that the Venezuelan paper received the article directly from Hugo Sassen and not via de *Gaceta Internacional*.
32 *VZ*, Dutch For. Min. to envoys in Paris, London, Berlin, Madrid and Washington, Sept. 4, 1875.
33 *VZ*, Wagner to Min. of Col., Aug. 21, 1875; Brakel to Dutch For. Min., Aug. 7, 1875.
34 The identity of Olavarría could not be established. He could be the Domingo A. Olavarría who participated in Guzmán Blanco's revolution of 1870, or José Antonio Alavarría. See Castellanos, pp. 151 and 413.
35 *VZ*, Brakel to Dutch For. Min., Aug. 7, 1875.
36 *VZ*, Brakel to Dutch For. Min., Sept. 20, 1875. Jesurun was already back in La Guaira without any results when Guzmán Blanco called him back. This occurred on Sept. 12.
37 *Ibid*.
38 *LA*, 1876, pp. 128-29. See also *VZ*, Brakel to Dutch For. Min., Aug. 18, 1875; Brakel to Blanco, Aug. 18, 1875; and Wagner to Min. of Col., Aug. 10, 1875.
39 *VZ*, Dutch For. Min. to Min. of Col., Sept. 23, 1875.

40   *VZ*, Brakel to Dutch For. Min., Aug. 31, Sept. 6, 1875. Rojas' letter with the Dutch demands arrived in Caracas at the end of August.
41   *VZ*, Dutch For. Min. to Brakel, Sept. 30, 1875. See also *FDdV*, I, 249, Rojas to Blanco, July 31, 1875, and *PHV*, 22, Blanco to Rojas, Sept. 6, 1875.
42   *Documents relatifs*, pp. 30-31; *LA*, 1876, pp. 129 ff. See also *VZ*, Rojas to Dutch For. Min., Oct. 1, 1875.
43   *VZ*, Blanco to Rojas, Sept. 6, 1875. See also *Documents relatifs*, p. 33 and *PHV*, 22, 29; Parra; *Doctrinas*, I, 172-73.
44   *VZ*, Dutch For. Min. to Rojas, Oct. 8, 1875; *Documents relatifs*, pp. 40-42.
45   *LA*, 1876, pp. 135-41, and *GO*, Nov. 25, 1875. See also *VZ*, Rojas to Dutch For. Min., Oct. 9, 1875; *Documents relatifs*, pp. 43-44; and *PHV*, 55 ff; and Parra, *Doctrinas*, I, 150-52.
46   *VZ*, Dutch For. Min. to Brakel, Oct. 9, 1875. The cable was sent to St. Thomas, brought from there to Curaçao by schooner and from this island by schooner to Venezuela. A similar procedure was used for Rojas' cables to Caracas.
47   *VZ*, Min. of Col. to Wagner, Oct. 15, 1875.

CHAPTER 12

1   *HTK*, II, 1875/76, pp. 1-3.
2   The *Midas* was returned Aug. 3, 1876, at St. Thomas, almost 2 years after its seizure.
3   *VZ*, Rojas to Dutch For. Min., Oct. 9, 1875.
4   *Diario de Avisos*, Sept. 7, 1875; *La Opinión Nacional*, Oct. 9, 1875: "El Jaque de Curaçao," Oct. 9, 1875: "Las Cosas de Curaçao." Oct. 21 and 22: "Nuestra Soberanía."
5   *VZ*, Van Bunge to Dutch envoy in Paris, Oct. 19, 1875. See also Woltring, II, 170-71.
6   *VZ*, Van Bunge to Dutch envoy in Paris, Oct. 23, 1875.
7   *VZ*, Van Bunge to Dutch envoy in Paris, Dec. 2, 1875.
8   *VZ*, Dutch For. Min. to envoys in London and Paris, Nov. 1, 1875.
9   *FDdV*, I, 273, Rojas to Blanco, Oct. 19, 1875. See also *PHV*, 138 and 173, Rojas to Blanco, Nov. 19 and Dec. 19, 1875.
10   Woltring, II, 174.
11   *VZ*, Von Bülow to German envoy in The Hague, Dec. 16, 1875; Dutch For. Min. to envoy in Berlin, Jan. 20, 1876. See also Woltring, II, 203. Brakel chose Stammann because the French minister had only just arrived in Caracas, the English minister was old, the Spanish did not like such a commission, and the American minister was too close to the Guzmán Blanco regime because of the planned marriage of his daughter to a relative of the president.
12   *VZ*, Dutch For. Min. to the king, Dec. 24, 1875; Stammann to Blanco, Nov. 29, 1875. Venezuela seems to have undertaken some steps to bring Von Bülow to this offer of arbitration. The Dutch were cautious. According to their For. Min. the Imperial Government had more than the usual interest in the conflict, and an evident desire to acquire Curaçao. See also Woltring, II, 203-7.
13   *VZ*, Dutch For. Min. to envoy in Washington, Oct. 29, 1875.
14   *VZ*, Dutch envoy in Washington to Dutch For. Min., Nov. 7 and Dec. 10, 1875.
15   *FDdV*, I, 273, Blanco to Rojas, Oct. 19, 1875; *VZ*, Dutch envoy in Paris to Dutch For. Min., Dec. 23, 1875.

16 *ON,* Oct. 22, 1875. See also *VZ,* Brakel to Dutch For. Min., Oct. 25, 1875; and *Foreign Relations,* 1875, pp. 1364-65.
17 *FDdV,* I, 250 ff., Blanco to Rojas, Aug. 4 and 12, 1875.
18 *FDdV,* II, 6, Blanco to Rojas, Oct. 4, 1875.
19 Woltring, II, 192-93, Minutes of a Cabinet meeting, Dec. 23, 1875.
20 *New York Tribune,* Nov. 18, 1875.
21 *ON,* Nov. 25 and 28, 1875. An interesting reaction came from a descendant of a Dutchman, living in Venezuela, who wrote to the Dutch For. Min.: "Est-ce possible que l'Hollande tolère pour plus longtemps l'hurlement de ces chiens?" He pointed out that Venezuela's only two coast guards did not deserve to be called men-of-war. *VZ,* Descendiente de un Holandés to Dutch For. Min., Oct. 4, 1875.
22 *VZ,* Dutch For. Min. to Brakel, Nov. 30, 1875.
23 *VZ,* Captain D. Heydeman to Dutch For. Min., Nov. 5, 1875.
24 *VZ,* Stammann to Von Bülow, Nov. 13, 1875; Blanco to Stammann, Nov. 19, 1875; *ON,* Nov. 25 and 28, 1875.
25 Corporaal, pp. 324-25.

CHAPTER 13

1 *VZ,* Dutch For. Min. to envoy in Brussels, July 3, 1875.
2 *Revue du Droit International,* 1875, pp. 710-11. See also Corporaal, p. 332.
3 *CC,* Aug. 11, 1875.
4 *CC,* Dec. 31, 1875. See also Corporaal, p. 332.
5 *KV,* Bijlage C, 1876/77, p. 127.
6 *GG,* XI, 35-37. See also *SP,* VI.
7 E. van Raalte, *Troonredes, openingsredes, inhuldigingsredes 1814-1963* ('s-Gravenhage, 1963), p. 152.
8 *HTK,* II, 1875/76, p. 6.
9 Woltring, II, 199, 214.
10 *GO,* May 29 and May 30, 1876. See also *VZ,* Blanco to Stammann, June 6, 1876; Stammann to Dutch For. Min., June 7, 1876.
11 *VZ,* Dutch envoy in London to Dutch For. Min., July 16, 1876; E. A. J. Harris, British envoy in The Hague to Dutch For. Min., July 17, 1876.
12 *VZ,* Dutch For. Min. to Min. of Col., July 22, 1876.
13 *VZ,* Stammann to Dutch For. Min., Aug. 26, 1876. The meeting took place Aug. 13: "Le 13 de ce mois, le soir, lorsque j'avais l'honneur d'un entretien avec Son Excellence le Président de la République, relativement à la goëlette *Midas,* Son Excellence profitait de cette occasion pour me parler de l'affaire des réclamations ..."
14 *VZ,* Stammann to Dutch For. Min., Nov. 5, 1876.
15 *VZ,* Memorandum de la Cuenta Internacional contra el Gobierno de Venezuela, n.d.
16 *VZ,* Stammann to Dutch For. Min., Sept. 4, 1876.
17 *VZ,* Canuto García to Stammann, Aug. 24, 1876: "Siendo la Ley de 29 de Mayo un acto del Congreso que él sólo puede derogar ... sin embargo procurando obviar la negativa de varias Legaciones el Presidente se ha decidido á hacer uso de la facultad constitucional que tiene para dirijir las negociaciones diplomáticas ..."
18 *VZ,* Dutch envoy in Washington to Dutch For. Min., Febr. 2, 1876. See also Woltring, II, 221-22.
19 *Ibid.,* II, 224.

20 *VZ*, Dutch envoy in Brussels to Dutch For. Min., Mar. 13, 1876.
21 Woltring, II, 237. See also *VZ*, Dutch envoy in Rome to Dutch For. Min., Mar. 15, 1876. The rumor was not true.
22 *VZ*, Pro Memory Note of the Cabinet chief Van Karnebeek, Apr. 1, 1876.
23 *Ibid.* See also Woltring, II, 245-47.
24 *Ibid.* See also *VZ*, Dutch envoy in Washington to Dutch For. Min., May 12, 1876.
25 *VZ*, Brakel to Dutch For. Min., Jun. 17, 1876.
26 *VZ*, Dutch envoy in Brussels to Dutch For. Min., Sept. 9, 1876.
27 *Ibid.* See also Woltring, II, 316-17.
28 *VZ*, Wagner to Min. of Col., Aug. 21, 1876.
29 *VZ*, Stammann to Dutch For. Min., Aug. 26, 1876: "... Schwierigkeiten mit den Zollbehörden dort gehabt habe und ihm Gegenstände an Bord confiskiert seien ... und kann nur hervorheben, dass die Zollbehörden in Puerto Cabello ganz den hiesigen Gesetzen gemäss und nicht in illegaler Weise gehandelt haben."
30 *St. Thomas Times,* Oct. 10, 1876. See also *VZ*, Dutch consul at St. Thomas to Dutch For. Min., Oct. 10, 1876.
31 *La Voz Pública,* Oct. 6, 1876. The expedition's goal was to support Báez in Santo Domingo.
32 *ON,* Oct. 6, 1876. The owner paid a fine of f. 3,700.
33 *VZ*, Wagner to Min. of Col., Oct. 7, 1876.
34 *VZ*, Stammann to Blanco, Apr. 5, 1876.
35 *Ibid.,* "... eigenmächtiges Verfahren."
36 *VZ*, Stammann to Dutch For. Min., Jul. 17, 1876. Stammann writes that the captain was received "auf die zuvorkommendste Weise" but told: "Kommen Sie nicht wieder, sonst halte ich Sie neunzig Tage."
37 *VZ*, Stamman to Dutch For. Min., July 6, 1876.
38 *VZ*, Stammann to Dutch For. Min., Jun. 13, 1876: "... mais c'est avec des chicanes dans les bureaux des douanes, avec des difficultés crées par l'interruption du télégraph etc. qu'on cherche à empêcher le traffic surtout entre Puerto Cabello et Curaçao." Stammann's correspondence is conducted partly in German, partly in French.
39 *Ibid.*
40 *VZ*, Dutch envoy in Paris to Dutch For. Min., Nov. 28, 1876. The envoy received his information from the Dutch consul in Paris, Martin Coster.
41 *Ibid.*
42 *VZ*, Brakel to Dutch For. Min., Nov. 21, 1876: "Concept Royal Decree" and "Toelichtende Nota" (Explanatory Note).
43 *HTK,* II, 1876/77, p. 395.
44 Corporaal, p. 335: "Deze verplichtingen ontstonden alleen, als er een oorlog tusschen twee Mogendheden gevoerd werd en het was hier slechts een kwestie van opstand geweest. Dit had de Minister onmiddellijk moeten constateren en hij had even hooghartig als de Venezolaansche gezant moeten verklaren, dat hij hierover niet in discussie kon treden."

CHAPTER 14

1 A. J. C. Krafft, ed., *Oranje en de zes Caraïbische Parelen* ('s-Gravenhage, 1948), pp. 256-57. See also Emmanuel, I, 412. The exact amount was 2,027,020 guilders.

2 This sum also includes the other five islands: Bonaire, Aruba, St. Martin, St. Eustatius, and Saba.

3 *CC,* Mar. 13, 1869.

4 Emmanuel, I, 411-12.

5 Cornelis Ch. Goslinga, "Van een diktator die Curaçao wilde kopen." *Oost en West,* L, 10 (October, 1957), pp. 12-15.

6 J. H. Adhin, "De immigratie van Hindustanen en de afstand van de Goudkust," *WIG* (1961), pp. 215-42. See also *HTK,* II, 1876/77, p. 400.

7 *HTK,* II, 1876/77, p. 400. See also Corporaal, p. 338.

8 *HTK,* II, 1876/77, p. 402 ff.

9 *CC,* Oct. 1, 1876: *St. Thomas Times,* Oct. 7, 1876.

10 *ON,* Oct. 31, 1876. See also *VZ,* Eduardo Calcaño, Ven. For. Min. to W. E. Boye, commercial agent of Venezuela in Curaçao, Oct. 30, 1876. The schooner brought 100 head of cattle, 100 *fánegas* corn, 50 quintal rice, 50 quintal coffee, and other items.

11 *VZ,* Dutch For. Min. to Stammann, Dec. 1, 1876: "Je vous prie vouloir bien témoigner tout d'abord de ma part à S.E. le Président des Etats Unis de Vénézuéla ma vive et sincère reconnaissance et de lui offrir l'hommage des sentiments de haute estime ..." Wagner wrote in similar terms.

12 Parra, *Doctrinas,* I, 263: Memoria de 1876. See also *CC,* Febr. 17, 1877, and Corporaal, p. 339.

13 *KV,* 1876, Bijlage C, 1876/77, p. 12.

14 *HTK,* II, 1876/77. Session of Friday, Dec. 1, 1876, pp. 395-403. One member of the Second Chamber, Vice-admiral Fabius, used strong words: "het prachtig ontslag" in terms of Wagner, and "zwendelaryen" in terms of the export of war materiel.

15 Corporaal, p. 342. Although the Dutch minister referred only to the Dutch press, the whole line of his defense seems to include the colonial and the Venezuelan press.

16 *PHV,* 80, 138, *et passim.* See also *VZ,* Dutch For. Min. to envoy in Paris, Jul. 24, 1877: Bijlage: Eigenhandige pro-memorie van de Minister van Buitenlandsche Zaken Van der Does de Willebois; and Woltring, II, 437-38.

17 *CC,* Febr. 10, 1877. This is discussed in an article entitled "De Kwestie van den Dag" (The Question of Today) by Ego (pseudonym of the Jewish/Dutch lawyer Eduard Isaac van Lier and others). See also *CC,* Febr. 17, 1877.

18 A. M. Chumaceiro, *Is Curaçao te koop?* (Den Haag, 1879), p. 15. Chumaceiro states that the colonial government received 10 cents on each imported and 10 cents on each exported rifle (p. 9). He strongly opposed the sale of the island and offered suggestions for its becoming self-supporting. See also *CC,* Mar. 24 and 29, 1877; *De Vrijmoedige,* Aug. 28, 1879, and Emmanuel, I, 413 and 446.

19 Woltring, II, 456.

20 *VZ,* Wagner to Min. of Col., Jan. 11, 1877.

21 *Min. de Hacienda,* Publication of Nov. 1876.

22 *VZ,* Wagner to Min. of Col., Oct. 1, 1877. See also Woltring, II, 455-67: Nota van den oud-gouverneur van Curaçao Wagner tot waardering en critiek der stukken indertijd door den Venezolaanschen gezant Rojas ingediend tot staving der vordering van Venezuela tot vergoeding der oorlogskosten door den opstand in de provincie Coro in 1874 veroorzaakt.

23 *NS,* May 14, 1877. These regulations were still in force in 1920.

24 The *escala* is a kind of port tax.

25 *GG,* XI, 209.

26 *FDdV,* I, 186, Rojas to Blanco, June 3, 1875.

27   *Ibid.*, I, 233 ff., Rojas to Blanco, July 7, 1875.
28   *GG*, IX, 210.
29   Corporaal, pp. 344-45.
30   *VZ*, Villanueva to Kip, Sept. 10, 1878.
31   *CC*, Dec. 29, 1877.
32   In *ARA* nor *MRE* proof could be found that "the affairs with Holland were in the process of being arranged," nor does Woltring, II, publish anything about it. See also *CC*, Mar. 16, 1878, and Corporaal, p. 345, who mentions a request by the American minister resident, Sept. 3, 1878, for the collaboration of the Netherlands in curbing the smuggling of war materiel to Venezuela.
33   *GG*, XI, 359 ff. The information on the Boulton House is given by Governor Kip in a letter to the Dutch Min. of Col., *VZ*, Mar. 29, 1879.
34   *GO*, Apr. 8, 1878. See also *ON*, May 27, 1878.
35   *VZ*, Min. of Col. to Dutch For. Min., Jun. 13, 1878.

CHAPTER 15

1   *CC*, Jul. 13, 1878.
2   See on this visit the report of Kip to Min. of Col., *VZ*, Febr. 21, 1879.
3   *VZ*, Dutch envoy in Paris to Dutch For. Min. ,Jan. 16, 1879. See also Woltring, II, 610.
4   *Nationale Zeitung*, Sept. 9, 1878. See also Woltring, II, 578; and *VZ*, Dutch envoy in Berlin to Dutch For. Min., Sept. 10, 1878.
5   *Nationale Zeitung*, Sept. 9, 1878. Erbwurst was translated with "pea sausage".
6   *VZ*, Private letter from Batavia to Dutch For. Min., Jan. 4, 1878.
7   *VZ*, Von Pestel to Dutch For. Min., Dec. 18, 1878.
8   Woltring, II, 610, n. 1.
9   *VZ*, Dutch envoy in Paris to Dutch For. Min., Jan. 16, 1879.
10   *VZ*, Dutch For. Min. to envoy in Paris, Jan. 23, 1879.
11   *VZ*, Dutch envoy in Paris to Dutch For. Min., Jan. 23, 1879.
12   *Ibid.* March 27, 1879.
13   *GG*, XII, 33: "... el vasto plan político que traía meditado ..."
14   *Ibid.*, pp. 36-37. See also Woltring, II, 615, n. 2.
15   *ON*, Jun. 4, 1879: "... para iniciar un arreglo que reduzca a la tercera parte la deuda exterior, para negociar tratados que liberten de derechos de importación en aquellos mercados los productos naturales de Venezuela, en cambio de la reciprocidad que otorgará a los productos naturales de aquellos países, y por último para formalizar la compra de Curaçao antes de proceder a la reorganización del sistema aduanero, asuntos todos de transcendental importancia para el progreso de nuestra Patria ..." See also *GO*, Jun. 3, 1879; and Foreign Relations, 1879/80, II, 1094. *GG*, XII, 61, calls the family issue 'un pretexto'."
16   *VZ*, Private letter, signed by L. Bloch to Martin Coster, Dutch consul-general in Paris, Febr. 7, 1879.
17   *GO*, Apr. 5, 1879. See also *VZ*, Kip to Min. of Col., Apr. 19, 1879; Dutch Min. of Col. to Dutch For. Min., May 20, 1879.
18   *VZ*, Ven. For. Min. to Kip, May 24, 1879.
19   Ybarra (or Ibarra) was engaged to the daughter of the American Minister Resident Thomas Russel, who was declared *persona non grata* by Guzmán Blanco. Ybarra was requested (or ordered) to break the engagement. He

refused and later married the young lady in question. See T. R. Ybarra, *Young Men of Caracas* (New York, 1941) p. 35.

20   *ON*, May 21, 1879. See also *GO*, May 23, 1879. The Venezuela publications were inspired by a column in the *Dagblad van Zuid-Holland en 's-Gravenhage*, Apr. 17, 1879, probably written by Hugo Sassen. The Hague was accused of a "falta absoluta de iniciación en el arreglo definitivo de la desagradable cuestión internacional en que ambas naciones se vieron seriamente comprometidas a consecuencia del procedor poco o nada fraternal de la colonia holandesa de Curaçao en las contiendas civiles de Venezuela."

21   *VZ*, Dutch For Min. to German envoy in The Hague, Sept. 6, 1879. See also Woltring, II, 664-66.

22   *VZ*, Dutch For. Min. to British envoy in The Hague, Dec. 13, 1879. There had been problems with the German Empire (on the *Carl Thorade*) with Great Britain (the *Magnet*), and two ships of the U.S.A.

23   *VZ*, Kip to Min. of Col., Sept. 4, 1879.

24   *El Imparcial*, Aug. 29, 1879.

25   *GG*, XII, 104.

26   *VZ*, Memorandum of the Chief of the Cabinet, Dec. 18, 1879. Willem Sassen was suspected to be the author of the hostile article in the *Dagblad van Zuid-Holland en 's-Gravenhage*, mentioned above and copied by *La Opinión Nacional*. See also Woltring, II, 755-57.

27   *VZ*, Min. of Marine to Dutch For. Min., Sept. 3, 1879; and Min. of Col. to Min. of Marine, Aug. 29, 1879.

28   There were again rumors that Venezuela was buying ironclads, but they turned out to be false. See *VZ*, Dutch For. Min. to Min. of Marine, Febr. 18, 1880.

29   Van Raalte, p. 157.

30   *NS*, Mar. 23 and 30, 1880. The blockade was lifted in February. See *ibid.*, May 22, 1880.

31   Rondón Márquez, I, 347.

32   *ON*, Febr. 20, 1880. We abridged somewhat the text.

33   *CC*, Mar. 13, 1880; and *VZ*, Dutch Min. of Col. to Dutch For. Min., May 28, 1880.

34   *VZ*, Kip to Min. of Col., Mar. 13, 1880.

35   Corporaal, p. 348.

36   De Jong, *Krimpende horizon*, pp. 71-75.

37   *Encyclopaedie van Nederlandsch West Indië* (Leiden/'s-Gravenhage, 1914, 1917), pp. 269-270.

38   Woltring, II, 801-2. See also *VZ*, Dutch envoy in London to Dutch For. Min., May 31, 1880.

39   Woltring, II, 905, n. 2.

40   *VZ*, For. Min. to Min. of Col., July 29, 1880. This affected especially the claims of Jeudah Senior.

41   *VZ*, Dutch envoy in Paris to Dutch For. Min., Oct. 1, 1880, refers to this arrangement, because of self-opiniated decreases in justified accounts as "perfidious actions." See also Dutch envoy in Berlin to For. Min., Jun. 29, 1880.

42   *VZ*, Memorandum of Ven. For. Ministry, May 13, 1880.

43   Harris, *Reluctant Diplomacy*, chapter V.

44   *VZ*, J. A. Jesurun to Dutch For. Min., Febr. 17, 1881.

45   *VZ*, Kip to Min. of Col., Sept. 17, 1880.

46   *VZ*, Kip to Ven. Min. of Col., Sept. 30, 1880. Among the expelled were such well-known men as León Colina, Fernando Adames, and Manuel M. Bermúdez.

47 *ON,* Oct. 1, 14, and 17, 1880. Guzmán Blanco sent General Jesús María
    Aristiguieta to Curaçao to accompany those refugees who had received
    amnesty back to Venezuela. See also *GG,* XII, 222.
48 *GG,* XII, 263.
49 Woltring, III, 56, n. 2.
50 *Ibid.* See also *VZ,* Dutch envoy in Paris to Dutch For. Min., July 15, 1881.
51 *VZ,* Van Heerdt to Min. of Col., Jul. 2, 1881. Kip was succeeded in Oct.
    1880 by Johannes H. A. W. van Heerdt tot Eversberg, if possible, even more
    colorless than his predecessor.
52 *ON,* Jun. 14, 1881.
53 Although there was talk of a Franco-Dutch alignment, it certainly never came
    that far. France was as reluctant as the Netherlands to use her military and
    naval power. See Woltring, III, pp. 84-86; 92-93; 105-106.
54 Corporaal, pp. 622-23. See also Parra, *Doctrinas,* II, 89-91; and *LA,* 1887,
    308, 315-17.
55 These protests touched upon a rather intricate judicial problem: can an
    agreement without a termination clause be denounced unilaterally?
56 *Foreign Relations,* 1882-83, pp. 523 ff. James G. Blaine to Geo. W. Carter,
    U. S. envoy in Caracas, Nov. 1, 1881.
57 Corporaal, pp. 355-56.
58 Emmanuel, I, 415.
59 *Ibdi.* See also *CC,* Jul. 22, 1887.
60 Ramón Azpurua, *Biografía de hombres notables de Hispano-América* (Cara-
    cas, 1877), II, 459-76. See also J. Hartog, *Brion* (Aruba, 1968), pp. 155-65.
61 *VZ,* Van Heerdt to Min. of Col., Oct. 2, 1881; Min. of Col. to Dutch For.
    Min., Nov. 1, 1881.
62 *LA,* 1883, pp. 148-77 gives the program, biographical notes on Brion, an
    ode dedicated to the Admiral by the Curaçao poet, J. H. B. Gravenhorst,
    and the correspondence between Willemstad and Caracas with regard to the
    celebration. The Governor of Curaçao chose as representatives the Attorney
    General and the commander of the Dutch naval forces stationed in Curaçao.
63 *VZ,* Seijas to Gov. of Cur., Oct. 7, 1881. The periodical in discussion was
    El Tribuno of short duration.
64 *VZ,* Seijas to Gov. of Cur., Nov. 21, 1881.
65 *VZ,* Van Heerdt to Min. of Col., Febr. 17, 1882.
66 *VZ,* Van Heerdt to Min. of Col., Febr. 21, 1882.
67 *VZ,* Van Heerdt to Min. of Col., Mar. 15, 1882.
68 Van Raalte, p. 159. This was said Sept. 18, 1882. It has the appearance of
    a deliberate attempt to hide the truth.
69 *VZ,* Dutch envoy in Wash. to Dutch For. Min., Dec. 4, 1882.
70 The U.S.A. had claims like many others powers. The members of a com-
    mittee to investigate those claims were accused of being bribed to inflate
    the amounts. See *Foreign Relations,* 1881-182, pp. 1199 ff.
71 *VZ,* Dutch For. Min. to Min. of Col., Apr. 12, 1883.
72 Van Raalte, p. 160.
73 Guzmán Blanco's message to Congress, Dec. 3, 1883. *GG,* XIII, 74.
74 *GG,* XIII, 75: "... expresa el buen estado en que se halla Venezuela con
    las naciones amigas." The articles in *El Imparcial* were written by Víctor
    Antonio Zerpa who wrote also an anti-Guzmán Blanco pamphlet: *Por la
    honra de Venezuela.*
75 Rojas, *Recuerdos,* xxvii.
76 Corporaal, pp. 358-59. The ship was later called *Guzmán Blanco.*
77 *VZ,* Dutch For. Min. to envoy in Paris, May 2, 1886.

78 He was appointed in Sept. 1882. His term ended in 1890.
79 Two other bridges were built during his term: one over the Waaigat, the other connecting the Molenplein with the Rif fortress in Otrabanda. See Hartog, *Curaçao*, II, 755.
80 *VZ*, Dutch For. Min. to Min. of Col., Oct. 7, 1886; Dutch For. Min. to Dutch consul in Caracas, Oct. 13, 1886. Consular activities were not affected by the break in diplomatic relations.
81 No written evidence of new negotiations was found.
82 *VZ*, Gov. of Cur. to Min. of Col., Sept. 2, 1886.
83 *VZ*, Gov. of Cur. to Guzmán Blanco, Apr. 20, 1886: "J'ose en même temps espérer que vous puissiez le trouver bon d'abolir les droits additionnels qui grèvent les marchandises originaires des Antilles à leur importation en Vénézuéla, une mesure qui, j'en suis sûr, contribuira beaucoup à renforcer les liens d'amitié qui unissent cette colonie à la République."
84 *GG*, XII, 413.
85 *GG*, XIII, 167 ff.
86 *VZ*, Diego B. Urbaneja to Gov. of Cur., Apr. 20, 1887.
87 *VZ*, Attorney General to Gov. of Cur., May 6, 1887; Van den Brandhof to Min. of Col., Aug. 16, 1887.
88 Emmanuel, I, 458-59: "*El Observador* ... while not a pronounced friend of the Catholics ... published sympathetic notes on Catholic life in Curaçao." Emmanuel should have added: "and unfriendly notes on Venezuela."
89 *VZ*, Van den Brandhof to Urbaneja, May 17, 1887.
90 *VZ*, Urbaneja to Van den Brandhof, Jun. 28, 1887.
91 *For. Rel.*, 1888, pp. 1636-37, Charles L. Scott to T. F. Bayard, Secr. of State, Sept. 3, 1887. See also *LA*, 1889, pp. 149-52.
92 *Ibid.* See also *VZ*, Van den Brandhof to Urbaneja (who was, however, since Aug. 1 replaced by Rafael Seijas), Aug. 15, 1887.
93 The date was postponed two weeks because of health reasons.
94 *VZ*, Boye to Van den Brandhof, Sept. 10, 1887.
95 *El Observador*, Aug. 23, 1887.
96 Obregón Silva complained about his expulsion in an open letter to the governor, Sept. 10, 1887.
97 *For. Rel.*, 1888, p. 1637. Scott gives some figures to indicate the size of this trade: In 1879 its value was almost $ 1,500,000. In 1884 it had increased to $ 2,953,000; in 1885 to $ 3,043,339. He estimated it over $ 4,000,000 for 1887.
98 *Ibid.*, Hermógenes López to Cleveland, May 7, 1888.
99 *Ibid.*, 1889, p. 717.
100 Lageman, *Recueil*, XII, 139-40. See appendix II; Parra, *Doctrinas*, II, 17-19, 277-78; and *La*, 1888, pp. 20-24; 1890, pp. 744-52; and 1895, pp. xliii, 166-67.

CHAPTER 16

1 Goslinga, "Papachi Sassen", *NWIG* (1968), p. 109.
2 *Ibid.*, p. 112.
3 A. M. Chumaceiro, *Is Curaçao te koop?* (Den Haag, 1879), pp. 19-20.
4 Lageman, *Recueil*, XII, 140.

BIBLIOGRAPHY

Adhin, J. H. "De immigratie van Hindustanen en de afstand van de Goudkust", *WIG* (1961), pp. 215-42.

Alvarado, Lisandro. *Historia de la Revolución Federal en Venezuela,* Caracas, 1956.

Amigo de las Antillas. *Het Nederlandsch-Venezolaansch Conflict,* Amsterdam, 1875.

Azpurua, Ramón. *Biografías de hombres notables de Hispano-América,* II, Caracas, 1877.

Bosch, Amry van den. *Dutch Foreign Policy Since 1815,* The Hague, 1959.

Bruzual, Manuel. *Los 'ilustres' o la estafa de los Guzmanes,* 3rd ed. Caracas, n.y.

Castellanos, Rafael R. *Guzmán Blanco íntimo,* Caracas, 1969.

Chumaceiro, A. M. *Is Curaçao te koop?* Den Haag, 1878.

Corporaal, Karel H. *De internationaalrechtelijke betrekkingen tusschen Nederland en Venezuela, 1816-1920,* Leiden, 1920.

Curaçaosche Courant, De.

Díaz Sánchez, Ramón. *Guzmán, elipse de una ambición de poder,* Caracas, 1954.

Emmanuel, Isaac S. and Suzanne A. *History of the Jews of the Netherlands Antilles,* 2 vols. Cincinnati, 1970.

Encyclopaedie van Nederlandsch West-Indië, Leiden-'s-Gravenhage, 1914-1917.

Eysinga, W. M. J. van. *Proeve eener inleiding tot het Nederlandsch tractatenrecht,* Leiden, 1907.

Foreign Relations of the United States.

Gaceta Oficial.

Gilmore, Robert L. *Caudillism and Militarism in Venezuela, 1810-1910,* Athens, Ohio, 1964.

González Guinán, Francisco. *Historia contemporánea de Venezuela,* 2nd ed. 15 vols., Caracas, 1954.

Goslinga, Cornelis Ch. "Van een diktator die Curaçao wilde kopen", *Oost en West,* L, 10 (October, 1957), pp. 12-15.
— "Papachi Sassen", *NWIG* (1968), pp. 105-49.

Handelingen van de Tweede Kamer der Staten Generaal.

Harris, William L. *The Reluctant Diplomacy of José María Rojas, 1873-1883,* Unpublished doctoral dissertation, University of Florida, Gainesville, 1973.

Hartog, J. *Curaçao,* vol. II, Oranjestad, 1961.
— *Brion,* Oranjestad, 1968.

Henríquez, José M. *Holanda y Venezuela. Refutación del folleto Venezuela y Holanda publicado por orden del Gobierno de Venezuela,* Curazao, 1876.

Hoetink, Harry. *Het patroon van de oude Curaçaose samenleving,* Assen, 1958.

Jong, Theo P. M. de. "Nederland en Latijns Amerika", *Economisch Historisch Jaarboek,* XXIX (1963), pp. 1-140.
— *De krimpende horizon van de Hollandse kooplieden,* Assen, 1966.

Koloniale Verslagen.

Krafft, A. J. C., ed., *Oranje en de zes Caraïbische parelen,* Amsterdam, 1948.

Lageman, E. G. *Recueil des traités et conventions conclus par le Royaume des Pays-Bas avec les puissances étrangères depuis 1813 jusqu'à nos jours,* Vol. VI and XII, La Haye, 1873, 1895.

Larrazábal, Felipe. *Ideario político y económico (1844-71),* 2nd ed. Caracas, 1963.
— *Guzmán Blanco. Restaurador del cadalso,* Curaçao, 1872.

Level de Goda, Francisco. *Historia contemporánea de Venezuela política y militar,* 2nd ed. 2 vols. Caracas, 1954.

Libro Amarillo de Venezuela, El.

Opinión Nacional, La.

Parra, Francisco J., ed. *Doctrinas de la Cancillería Venezolana. Digesto,* 2 vols. New York, 1952-53.

Pensamiento político venezolano del siglo XIX, V and VI, *La Doctrina Liberal. Antonio Leocadio Guzmán,* 2 vols. Caracas, 1961.

Pool, John de. *Del Curaçao que se va,* Santiago de Chile, 1935.

Raalte, E. van. *Troonredes, openingsredes, inhuldigingsredes, 1814-1963,* 's-Gravenhage, 1963.

Ralston, J. H. *International Arbitral Law and Procedure,* New York, 1910.

Rojas, José María de. *Recuerdos de la patria,* 2nd ed. Caracas, 1963.
— *Het Nederlandsch Venezolaansch Conflict,* Brussels, 1875.

Rondón Márquez, Rafael A. *Guzmán Blanco. El autócrata civilizador,* 2 vols., Caracas, 1944.

Tratados públicos y acuerdos internacionales de Venezuela. 2nd ed., I, Caracas, 1951.

Vénézuéla et les Pays-Bas. Documents relatifs à la rupture des rapports officiels entre les Gouvernements de Vénézuéla et des Pays-Bas, Paris, 1875.

Wise, George S. *Caudillo. A Portrait of Guzmán Blanco,* New York, 1951.

Woltring, J. ed. *Bescheiden betreffende de buitenlandse politiek van Nederland, 1848-1919,* 3 vols., 's-Gravenhage, 1962-67.

Ybarra, T. R. *Young Men of Caracas,* New York, 1941.

Zerpa, Victor A. *Por la honra de Venezuela,* Curaçao, 1884.

GENERAL INDEX

Printed in the United States
By Bookmasters